The

CLASSIC WORKS

of

A. W. TOZER

The Pursuit of God

&

Man - The Dwelling Place of God

CONTENTS

THE
PURSUIT
OF
GOD

INTRODUCTION

Here is a masterly study of the inner life by a heart thirsting after God, eager to grasp at least the outskirts of His ways, the abyss of His love for sinners, and the height of His unapproachable majesty—and it was written by a busy pastor in Chicago!

Who could imagine David writing the twenty-third Psalm on South Halsted Street, or a medieval mystic finding inspiration in a small study on the second floor of a frame house on that vast, flat checker-board of endless streets

> *Where cross the crowded ways of life*
> *Where sound the cries of race and clan,*
> *In haunts of wretchedness and need,*
> *On shadowed threshold dark with fears,*
> *And paths where hide the lures of greed ...*

But even as Dr. Frank Mason North, of New York, says in his immortal poem, so Mr. Tozer says in this book:

> *Above the noise of selfish strife*
> *We hear Thy voice, O Son of Man.*

My acquaintance with the author is limited to brief visits and loving fellowship in his church. There I discovered a self-made scholar, an omnivorous reader with a remarkable library of theological and devotional books, and one who seemed to burn the midnight oil in pursuit of God. His book is the result of long meditation and much prayer. It is not a collection of sermons. It does not deal with the pulpit and the pew but with the soul athirst for God. The chapters could be summarized in Moses'

[handwritten margin notes: Ex. 33:18 — God's presence; Romans 11:33-36 — doxology; prayer for God's power]

prayer, "Show me thy glory," or Paul's exclamation, "O the depth of the riches both of the wisdom and knowledge of God!" It is theology not of the head but of the heart.

There is deep insight, sobriety of style, and a catholicity of outlook that is refreshing. The author has few quotations but he knows the saints and mystics of the centuries—Augustine, Nicholas of Cusa, Thomas à Kempis, von Hügel, Finney, Wesley and many more. The ten chapters are heart searching and the prayers at the close of each are for closet, not pulpit. *I felt the nearness of God while reading them.*

Here is a book for every pastor, missionary, and devout Christian. It deals with the deep things of God and the riches of His grace. Above all, it has the keynote of sincerity and humility.

Samuel M. Zwemer
New York City

[handwritten note:]
Romans 11:32
"For God has bound all men over to disobedience so that he may have mercy on them all."
I struggle with this - makes us look like "playthings" and we have no choice.??

PREFACE

In this hour of all-but-universal darkness one cheering gleam appears: within the fold of conservative Christianity there are to be found increasing numbers of persons whose religious lives are marked by a growing hunger after God Himself. They are eager for spiritual realities and will not be put off with words, nor will they be content with correct "interpretations" of truth. They are athirst for God, and they will not be satisfied till they have drunk deep at the Fountain of Living Water.

This is the only real harbinger of revival which I have been able to detect anywhere on the religious horizon. It may be the cloud the size of a man's hand for which a few saints here and there have been looking. It can result in a resurrection of life for many souls and a recapture of that radiant wonder which should accompany faith in Christ, that wonder which has all but fled the Church of God in our day.

But this hunger must be recognized by our religious leaders. Current evangelicalism has (to change the figure) laid the altar and divided the sacrifice into parts, but now seems satisfied to count the stones and rearrange the pieces with never a care that there is not a sign of fire upon the top of lofty Carmel. But God be thanked that there are a few who care. They are those who, while they love the altar and delight in the sacrifice, are yet unable to reconcile themselves to the continued absence of fire. They desire God above all. They are athirst to taste for themselves the "piercing sweetness" of the love of Christ about Whom all the holy prophets did write and the psalmists did sing.

There is today no lack of Bible teachers to set forth correctly the principles of the doctrines of Christ, but too many of these seem satisfied to teach the fundamentals of the faith year after year, strangely unaware that there is in their ministry no manifest Presence, nor anything unusual in their personal lives. They minister constantly to believers who feel within their breasts a longing which their teaching simply does not satisfy.

I trust I speak in charity, but the lack in our pulpits is real. Milton's terrible sentence applies to our day as accurately as it did to his: "The hungry sheep look up, and are not fed." It is a solemn thing, and no small scandal in the Kingdom, to see God's children starving while actually seated at the Father's table. The truth of Wesley's words is established before our eyes: "Orthodoxy, or right opinion, is, at best, a very slender part of religion. Though right tempers cannot subsist without right opinions, yet right opinions may subsist without right tempers. There may be a right opinion of God without either love or one right temper toward Him. Satan is a proof of this."

Thanks to our splendid Bible societies and to other effective agencies for the dissemination of the Word, there are today many millions of people who hold "right opinions," probably more than ever before in the history of the Church. Yet I wonder if there was ever a time when true spiritual worship was at a lower ebb. To great sections of the Church the art of worship has been lost entirely, and in its place has come that strange and foreign thing called the "program." This word has been borrowed from the stage and applied with sad wisdom to the type of public service which now passes for worship among us.

Sound Bible exposition is an imperative *must* in the Church of the Living God. Without it no church can be a New Testament church in any strict meaning of that term. But exposition may be carried on in such way as to leave the hearers devoid of any true spiritual nourishment whatever. For it is not mere words that nourish the soul, but God Himself, and unless and until the hearers find God in personal experience they are not the better for having heard the truth. The Bible is not an end in itself, but a means to bring men to an intimate and satisfying knowledge of God, that they may enter into Him, that they may delight in His Presence, may taste and know the inner sweetness of the very God Himself in the core and center of their hearts.

This book is a modest attempt to aid God's hungry children so to find Him. Nothing here is new except in the sense that it is a discovery which my own heart has made of spiritual realities most delightful and wonderful to me. Others before me have gone much farther into these holy mysteries than I have done, but if my fire is not large it is yet real, and there may be those who can light their candle at its flame.

A. W. Tozer
Chicago, Ill.
June 16, 1948

1
FOLLOWING HARD AFTER GOD

My soul followeth hard after thee: thy right hand up-
holdeth me.—Psa. 63:8

Christian theology teaches the doctrine of prevenient grace, which briefly stated means this, that before a man can seek God, God must first have sought the man.

Before a sinful man can think a right thought of God, there must have been a work of enlightenment done within him; imperfect it may be, but a true work nonetheless, and the secret cause of all desiring and seeking and praying which may follow.

We pursue God because, and only because, He has first put an urge within us that spurs us to the pursuit. "No man can come to me," said our Lord, "except the Father which hath sent me draw him," and it is by this very prevenient *drawing* that God takes from us every vestige of credit for the act of coming. The impulse to pursue God originates with God, but the outworking of that impulse is our following hard after Him; and all the time we are pursuing Him we are already in His hand: "Thy right hand upholdeth me."

In this divine "upholding" and human "following" there is no contradiction. All is of God, for as von Hügel teaches, *God is always previous*. In practice, however, (that is, where God's previous working meets man's present response) man must pursue God. On our part there must be positive reciprocation if this secret drawing of God is to eventuate in identifiable experience of the Divine. In the warm language of personal feeling this is stated in the Forty-second Psalm: "As the hart panteth after the water brooks, so panteth my soul after thee, O God. My soul thirsteth for God, for the living God: when shall I come and appear before God?" This is deep calling unto deep, and the longing heart will understand it.

The doctrine of justification by faith—a Biblical truth, and a blessed relief from sterile legalism and unavailing self-effort—has in our time fallen into evil company and been interpreted by many in such manner as actually to bar men from the knowledge of God. The whole transaction of religious conversion has been made mechanical and spiritless. Faith may now be exercised without a jar to the moral life and without embarrassment to the Adamic ego. Christ may be "received" without creating any special love for Him in the soul of the receiver. The man is "saved," but he is not hungry nor thirsty after God. In fact he is specifically taught to be satisfied and encouraged to be content with little.

The modern scientist has lost God amid the wonders of His world; we Christians are in real danger of losing God amid the wonders of His Word. We have almost forgotten that God is a Person and, as such, can be cultivated as any person can. It is inherent in personality to be able to know other personalities, but full knowledge of one personality by another cannot be achieved in one encounter. It is only after long and loving mental intercourse that the full possibilities of both can be explored.

All social intercourse between human beings is a response of personality to personality, grading upward from the most casual brush between man and man to the fullest, most intimate communion of which the human soul is capable. Religion, so far as it is genuine, is in essence the response of created personalities to the Creating Personality, God. "This is life eternal, that they might know thee the only true God, and Jesus Christ, whom thou hast sent."

God is a Person, and in the deep of His mighty nature He thinks, wills, enjoys, feels, loves, desires and suffers as any other person may. In making Himself known to us He stays by the familiar pattern of personality. He communicates with us through the avenues of our minds, our wills and our emotions. The continuous and unembarrassed interchange of love and thought between God and the soul of the redeemed man is the throbbing heart of New Testament religion.

This intercourse between God and the soul is known to us in conscious personal awareness. It is personal: that is, it does not come through the body of believers, as such, but is known to the individual, and to the body through the individuals which compose it. And it is conscious: that is, it does not stay below the threshold of consciousness and work there unknown to the soul (as, for instance, infant baptism is thought by some to do), but comes within the field of awareness where the man can "know" it as he knows any other fact of experience.

You and I are in little (our sins excepted) what God is in large. Being made in His image we have within us the capacity to know Him. In our sins we lack only the power. The moment the Spirit has quickened us to life in regeneration our whole being senses its kinship to God and leaps up in joyous recognition. That is the heavenly birth without which we cannot see the Kingdom of God. It is, however, not an end but an inception, for now begins the glorious pursuit, the heart's happy exploration of the infinite riches of the Godhead. That is where we begin, I say, but where we stop no man has yet discovered, for there is in the awful and mysterious depths of the Triune God neither limit nor end.

Shoreless Ocean, who can sound Thee?
Thine own eternity is round Thee,
Majesty divine!

To have found God and still to pursue Him is the soul's paradox of love, scorned indeed by the too-easily-satisfied religionist, but justified in happy experience by the children of the burning heart. St. Bernard stated this holy paradox in a musical quatrain that will be instantly understood by every worshipping soul:

We taste Thee, O Thou Living Bread,
And long to feast upon Thee still:
We drink of Thee, the Fountainhead
And thirst our souls from Thee to fill.

Come near to the holy men and women of the past and you will soon feel the heat of their desire after God. They mourned for Him, they prayed and wrestled and sought for Him day and night, in season and out, and when they had found Him the finding was all the sweeter for the long seeking. Moses used the fact that he knew God as an argument for knowing Him better. "Now, therefore, I pray thee, if I have found grace in thy sight, show me now thy way, that I may know thee, that I may find grace in thy sight"; and from there he rose to make the daring request,

"I beseech thee, show me thy glory." God was frankly pleased by this display of ardor, and the next day called Moses into the mount, and there in solemn procession made all His glory pass before him.

David's life was a torrent of spiritual desire, and his psalms ring with the cry of the seeker and the glad shout of the finder. Paul confessed the mainspring of his life to be his burning desire after Christ. "That I may know Him," was the goal of his heart, and to this he sacrificed everything. "Yea doubtless, and I count all things but loss for the excellency of the knowledge of Christ Jesus my Lord: for whom I have suffered the loss of all things, and do count them but refuse, that I may win Christ."

Hymnody is sweet with the longing after God, the God whom, while the singer seeks, he knows he has already found. "His track I see and I'll pursue," sang our fathers only a short generation ago, but that song is heard no more in the great congregation. How tragic that we in this dark day have had our seeking done for us by our teachers. Everything is made to center upon the initial act of "accepting" Christ (a term, incidentally, which is not found in the Bible) and we are not expected thereafter to crave any further revelation of God to our souls. We have been snared in the coils of a spurious logic which insists that if we have found Him we need no more seek Him. This is set before us as the last word in orthodoxy, and it is taken for granted that no Bible-taught Christian ever believed otherwise. Thus the whole testimony of the worshipping, seeking, singing Church on that subject is crisply set aside. The experiential heart-theology of a grand army of fragrant saints is rejected in favor of a smug interpretation of Scripture which would certainly have sounded strange to an Augustine, a Rutherford or a Brainerd.

In the midst of this great chill there are some, I rejoice to acknowledge, who will not be content with shallow logic. They will admit the force of the argument, and then turn away with tears to hunt some lonely place and pray, "O God, show me thy glory." They want to taste, to touch with their hearts, to see with their inner eyes the wonder that is God.

I want deliberately to encourage this mighty longing after God. The lack of it has brought us to our present low estate. The stiff and wooden quality about our religious lives is a result of our lack of holy desire. Complacency is a deadly foe of all spiritual growth. Acute desire must be present or there will be no manifestation of Christ to His people. He waits to be wanted. Too bad that with many of us He waits so long, so very long, in vain.

Every age has its own characteristics. Right now we are in an age of religious complexity. The simplicity which is in Christ is rarely found among us. In its stead are programs, methods, organizations and a world of nervous activities which occupy time and attention but can never satisfy the longing of the heart. The shallowness of our inner experience, the hollowness of our worship, and that servile imitation of the world which marks our promotional methods all testify that we, in this day, know God only imperfectly, and the peace of God scarcely at all.

If we would find God amid all the religious externals we must first determine to find Him, and then proceed in the way of simplicity. Now as always God discovers Himself to "babes" and hides Himself in thick darkness from the wise and the prudent. We must simplify our approach to Him. We must strip down to essentials (and they will be found to be blessedly few). We must put away all effort to impress, and come with the guileless candor of childhood. If we do this, without doubt God will quickly respond.

When religion has said its last word, there is little that we need other than God Himself. The evil habit of seeking *God-and* effectively prevents us from finding God in full revelation. In the "and" lies our great woe. If we omit the "and" we shall soon find God, and in Him we shall find that for which we have all our lives been secretly longing.

We need not fear that in seeking God only we may narrow our lives or restrict the motions of our expanding hearts. The opposite is true. We can well afford to make God our All, to concentrate, to sacrifice the many for the One.

The author of the quaint old English classic, *The Cloud of Unknowing*, teaches us how to do this. "Lift up thine heart unto God with a meek stirring of love; and mean Himself, and none of His goods. And thereto, look thee loath to think on aught but God Himself. So that nought work in thy wit, nor in thy will, but only God Himself. This is the work of the soul that most pleaseth God."

Again, he recommends that in prayer we practice a further stripping down of everything, even of our theology. "For it sufficeth enough, a naked intent direct unto God without any other cause than Himself." Yet underneath all his thinking lay the broad foundation of New Testament truth, for he explains that by "Himself" he means "God that made thee, and bought thee, and that graciously called thee to thy degree." And he is all for simplicity: If we would have religion "lapped and folden in one word, for that thou shouldst have better hold thereupon, take thee but a little word of one syllable: for so it is better than of two, for even the shorter it is the better it accordeth with the work of the Spirit. And such a word is this word GOD or this word LOVE."

When the Lord divided Canaan among the tribes of Israel Levi received no share of the land. God said to him simply, "I am thy part and thine inheritance," and by those words made him richer than all his brethren, richer than all the kings and rajas who have ever lived in the world. And there is a spiritual principle here, a principle still valid for every priest of the Most High God.

The man who has God for his treasure has all things in One. Many ordinary treasures may be denied him, or if he is allowed to have them, the enjoyment of them will be so tempered that they will never be necessary to his happiness. Or if he must see them go, one after one, he will scarcely feel a sense of loss, for having the Source of all things he has in One all satisfaction, all pleasure, all delight. Whatever he may lose he has actually lost nothing, for he now has it all in One, and he has it purely, legitimately and forever.

* * *

O God, I have tasted Thy goodness, and it has both satisfied me and made me thirsty for more. I am painfully conscious of my need of further grace. I am ashamed of my lack of desire. O God, the Triune God, I want to want Thee; I long to be filled with longing; I thirst to be made more thirsty still. Show me Thy glory, I pray Thee, that so I may know Thee indeed. Begin in mercy a new work of love within me. Say to my soul, "Rise up, my love, my fair one, and come away." Then give me grace to rise and follow Thee up from this misty lowland where I have wandered so long.

In Jesus' Name, Amen.

2
THE BLESSEDNESS OF POSSESSING NOTHING

Blessed are the poor in spirit: for theirs is the kingdom of heaven.—Matt. 5:3

Before the Lord God made man upon the earth He first prepared for him by creating a world of useful and pleasant things for his sustenance and delight. In the Genesis account of the creation these are called simply "things." They were made for man's uses, but they were meant always to be external to the man and subservient to him. In the deep heart of the man was a shrine where none but God was worthy to come. Within him was God; without, a thousand gifts which God had showered upon him.

But sin has introduced complications and has made those very gifts of God a potential source of ruin to the soul.

Our woes began when God was forced out of His central shrine and "things" were allowed to enter. Within the human heart "things" have taken over. Men have now by nature no peace within their hearts, for God is crowned there no longer, but there in the moral dusk stubborn and aggressive usurpers fight among themselves for first place on the throne.

This is not a mere metaphor, but an accurate analysis of our real spiritual trouble. There is within the human heart a tough fibrous root of fallen life whose nature is to possess, always to possess. It covets "things" with a deep and fierce passion. The pronouns "my" and "mine" look innocent enough in print, but their constant and universal use is significant. They express the real nature of the old Adamic man better than a thousand volumes of theology could do. They are verbal symptoms of our deep disease. The roots of our hearts have grown down into *things*, and we dare not pull up one rootlet lest we die. Things have become necessary to us, a development never originally intended. God's gifts now take the place of God, and the whole course of nature is upset by the monstrous substitution.

Our Lord referred to this tyranny of *things* when He said to His disciples, "If any man will come after me, let him deny himself, and take up his cross, and follow me. For whosoever will save his life shall lose it: and whosoever shall lose his life for my sake shall find it." *how often do we lose life for other reasons?*

Breaking this truth into fragments for our better understanding, it would seem that there is within each of us an enemy which we tolerate at our peril. Jesus called it "life" and "self," or as we would say, the *self-life*. Its chief characteristic is its possessiveness: the words "gain" and "profit" suggest this. To allow this enemy to live is in the end to lose everything. To repudiate it and give up all for Christ's sake is to lose nothing at last, but to preserve everything unto life eternal. And possibly also a hint is given here as to the only effective way to destroy this foe: it is by the Cross. "Let him take up his cross and follow me."

The way to deeper knowledge of God is through the lonely valleys of soul poverty and abnegation of all things. The blessed ones who possess the Kingdom are they who have repudiated every external thing and have rooted from their hearts all sense of possessing. These are the "poor in spirit." They have reached an inward state paralleling the outward circumstances of the common beggar in the streets of Jerusalem; that is what the word "poor" as Christ used it actually means. These blessed poor are no longer slaves to the tyranny of *things*. They have broken the yoke of the oppressor; and this they have done not by fighting but by surrendering. Though free from all sense of possessing, they yet possess all things. "Theirs is the kingdom of heaven."

Let me exhort you to take this seriously. It is not to be understood as mere Bible teaching to be stored away in the mind along with an inert mass of other doctrines. It is a marker on the road to greener pastures, a path chiseled against the steep sides of the mount of God. We dare not try to by-pass it if we would follow on in this holy pursuit. We must ascend a step at a time. If we refuse one step we bring our progress to an end.

As is frequently true, this New Testament principle of spiritual life finds its best illustration in the Old Testament. In the story of Abraham and Isaac we have a dramatic picture of the surrendered life as well as an excellent commentary on the first Beatitude.

Abraham was old when Isaac was born, old enough indeed to have been his grandfather, and the child became at once the delight and idol of his heart. From that moment when he first stooped to take the tiny form awkwardly in his arms he was an eager love slave of his son. God went out of His way to comment on the strength of this affection. And it is not hard to understand. The baby represented everything sacred to his father's heart: the promises of God, the covenants, the hopes of the years and the long messianic dream. As he watched him grow from babyhood to young manhood the heart of the old man was knit closer and closer with the life of his son, till at last the relationship bordered upon the perilous. It was then that God stepped in to save both father and son from the consequences of an uncleansed love.

"Take now thy son," said God to Abraham, "thine only son Isaac, whom thou lovest, and get thee into the land of Moriah; and offer him there for a burnt-offering upon one of the mountains which I will tell thee of." The sacred writer spares us a close-up of the agony that night on the slopes near Beersheba when the aged man had it out with his God, but respectful imagination may view in awe the bent form and convulsive wrestling alone under the stars. Possibly not again until a Greater than Abraham wrestled in the Garden of Gethsemane did such mortal pain visit a human soul. If only the man himself might have been allowed to die. That would have been easier a thousand times, for he was old now, and to die would have been no great ordeal for one who had walked so long with God. Besides, it would have been a last sweet pleasure to let his dimming vision rest upon the figure of his stalwart son who would live to carry on the Abrahamic line and fulfill in himself the promises of God made long before in Ur of the Chaldees.

How should he slay the lad! Even if he could get the consent of his wounded and protesting heart, how could he reconcile the act with the promise, "In Isaac shall thy seed be called"? This was Abraham's trial by fire, and he did not fail in the crucible. While the stars still shone like sharp white points above the tent where the sleeping Isaac lay, and long before the gray dawn had begun to lighten the east, the old saint had made up his mind. He would offer his son as God had directed him to do, and *then trust God to raise him from the dead*. This, says the writer to the Hebrews, was the solution his aching heart found sometime in the dark night, and he rose "early in the morning" to carry out the plan. It is beautiful to see that, while he erred as to God's method, he had correctly sensed the secret of His great heart. And the solution accords well with the New Testament Scripture, "Whosoever will lose for my sake shall find."

God let the suffering old man go through with it up to the point where He knew there would be no retreat, and then forbade him to lay a hand upon the boy. To the wondering patriarch He now says in effect, "It's all right, Abraham. I never intended that you should actually slay the lad. I only wanted to remove him from the temple of your heart that I might reign unchallenged there. I wanted to correct the perversion that existed in your love. Now you may have the boy, sound and well. Take him and go back to your tent. Now I know that thou fearest God, seeing that thou hast not withheld thy son, thine only son, from me."

Then heaven opened and a voice was heard saying to him, "By myself have I sworn, saith the Lord, for because thou hast done this thing, and hast not withheld thy son, thine only son: that in blessing I will bless thee, and in multiplying I will multiply thy seed as the stars of the heaven, and as the sand which is upon the sea shore; and thy seed shall possess the gate of his enemies; and in thy seed shall all the nations of the earth be blessed; because thou hast obeyed my voice."

The old man of God lifted his head to respond to the Voice, and stood there on the mount strong and pure and grand, a man marked out by the Lord for special treatment, a friend and favorite of the Most High. Now he was a man wholly surrendered, a man utterly obedient, a man who possessed nothing. He had concentrated his all in the person of his dear son, and God had taken it from him. God could have begun out on the margin of Abraham's life and worked inward to the center; He chose rather to cut quickly to the heart and have it over in one sharp act of separation. In dealing thus He practiced an economy of means and time. It hurt cruelly, but it was effective.

I have said that Abraham possessed nothing. Yet was not this poor man rich? Everything he had owned before was his still to enjoy: sheep, camels, herds, and goods of every sort. He had also his wife and his friends, and best of all he had his son Isaac safe by his side. He had everything, but *he possessed nothing*. There is the spiritual secret. There is the sweet theology of the heart which can be learned only in the school of renunciation. The books on systematic theology overlook this, but the wise will understand.

After that bitter and blessed experience I think the words "my" and "mine" never had again the same meaning for Abraham. The sense of possession which they connote was gone from his heart. *Things* had been cast out forever. They had now become external to the man. His inner heart was free from them. The world said, "Abraham is rich," but the aged patriarch only smiled. He could not explain it to them, but he knew that he owned nothing, that his real treasures were inward and eternal.

There can be no doubt that this possessive clinging to things is one of the most harmful habits in the life. Because it is so natural it is rarely recognized for the evil that it is; but its outworkings are tragic.

We are often hindered from giving up our treasures to the Lord out of fear for their safety; this is especially true when those treasures are loved relatives and friends. But we need have no such fears. Our Lord came not to destroy but to save. Everything is safe which we commit to Him, and nothing is really safe which is not so committed.

Our gifts and talents should also be turned over to Him. They should be recognized for what they are, God's loan to us, and should never be considered in any sense our own. We have no more right to claim credit for special abilities than for blue eyes or strong muscles. "For who maketh thee to differ from another? and what hast thou that thou didst not receive?"

The Christian who is alive enough to know himself even slightly will recognize the symptoms of this possession malady, and will grieve to find them in his own heart. If the longing after God is strong enough within him he will want to do something about the matter. Now, what should he do?

First of all he should put away all defense and make no attempt to excuse himself either in his own eyes or before the Lord. Whoever defends himself will have himself for his defense, and he will have no other; but let him come defenseless before the Lord and he will have for his defender no less than God Himself. Let the inquiring Christian trample under foot every slippery trick of his deceitful heart and insist upon frank and open relations with the Lord.

Then he should remember that this is holy business. No careless or casual dealings will suffice. Let him come to God in full determination to be heard. Let him insist that God accept his all, that He take *things* out of his heart and Himself reign there in power. It may be he will need to become specific, to name things and people by their names one by one. If he will become drastic enough he can shorten the time of his travail from years to minutes and enter the good land long before his slower brethren who coddle their feelings and insist upon caution in their dealings with God.

Let us never forget that such a truth as this cannot be learned by rote as one would learn the facts of physical science. They must be *experienced* before we can really know them. We must in our hearts live through Abraham's harsh and bitter experiences if we would know the blessedness which follows them. The ancient curse will not go out painlessly; the tough old miser within us will not lie down and die obedient to our command. He must be torn out of our heart like a plant from the soil; he must be extracted in agony and blood like a tooth from the jaw. He must be expelled from our soul by violence as Christ expelled the money changers from the temple. And we shall need to steel ourselves against his piteous begging, and to recognize it as springing out of self-pity, one of the most reprehensible sins of the human heart.

If we would indeed know God in growing intimacy we must go this way of renunciation. And if we are set upon the pursuit of God He will sooner or later bring us to this test. Abraham's testing was, at the time, not known to him as such, yet if he had taken some course other than the one he did, the whole history of the Old Testament would have been different. God would have found His man, no doubt, but the loss to Abraham would have been tragic beyond the telling. So we will be brought one by one to the testing place, and we may never know when we are there. At that testing place there will be no dozen possible choices for us; just one and an alternative, but our whole future will be conditioned by the choice we make.

* * *

Father, I want to know Thee, but my coward heart fears to give up its toys. I cannot part with them without inward bleeding, and I do not try to hide from Thee the terror of the parting. I come trembling, but I do come. Please root from my heart all those things which I have cherished so long and which have become a very part of my living self, so that Thou mayest enter and dwell there without a rival. Then shalt Thou make the place of Thy feet glorious. Then shall my heart have no need of the sun to shine in it, for Thyself wilt be the light of it, and there shall be no night there.

In Jesus' Name, Amen.

3
REMOVING THE VEIL

Having therefore, brethren, boldness to enter into the
holiest by the blood of Jesus.—Heb. 10:19

Among the famous sayings of the Church fathers none is better known than Augustine's, "Thou hast formed us for Thyself, and our hearts are restless till they find rest in Thee."

The great saint states here in few words the origin and interior history of the human race. God made us for Himself: that is the only explanation that satisfies the *heart* of a thinking man, whatever his wild reason may say. Should faulty education and perverse reasoning lead a man to conclude otherwise, there is little that any Christian can do for him. For such a man I have no message. My appeal is addressed to those who have been previously taught in secret by the wisdom of God: I speak to thirsty hearts whose longings have been wakened by the touch of God within them, and such as they need no reasoned proof. Their restless hearts furnish all the proof they need.

God formed us for Himself. The *Shorter Catechism*, "Agreed upon by the Reverend Assembly of Divines at Westminster," as the old *New-England Primer* has it, asks the ancient questions *what* and *why* and answers them in one short sentence hardly matched in any uninspired work. "*Question*: What is the chief End of Man? *Answer:* Man's chief End is to glorify God and enjoy Him forever." With this agree the four and twenty elders who fall on their faces to worship Him that liveth for ever and ever, saying, "Thou art worthy, O Lord, to receive glory and honour and power: for thou hast created all things, and for thy pleasure they are and were created."

God formed us for His pleasure, and so formed us that we as well as He can in divine communion enjoy the sweet and mysterious mingling of kindred personalities. He meant us to see Him and live with Him and draw our life from His smile. But we have been guilty of that "foul revolt" of which Milton speaks when describing the rebellion of Satan and his hosts. We have broken with God. We have ceased to obey Him or love Him and in guilt and fear have fled as far as possible from His Presence.

Yet who can flee from His Presence when the heaven and the heaven of heavens cannot contain Him? when as the wisdom of Solomon testifies, "the Spirit of the Lord filleth the world?" The omnipresence of the Lord is one thing, and is a solemn fact necessary to His perfection; the *manifest* Presence is another thing altogether, and from that Presence we have fled, like Adam, to hide among the trees of the garden, or like Peter to shrink away crying, "Depart from me, for I am a sinful man, O Lord."

So the life of man upon the earth is a life away from the Presence, wrenched loose from that "blissful center" which is our right and proper dwelling place, our first estate which we kept not, the loss of which is the cause of our unceasing restlessness.

The whole work of God in redemption is to undo the tragic effects of that foul revolt, and to bring us back again into right and eternal relationship with Himself. This required that our sins be disposed of satisfactorily, that a full reconciliation be effected and the way opened for us to return again into conscious communion with God and to live again in the Presence as before. Then by His prevenient working within us He moves us to return. This first comes to our notice when our restless hearts feel a yearning for the Presence of God and we say within ourselves, "I will arise and go to my Father." That is the first step, and as the Chinese sage Lao-tze has said, "The journey of a thousand miles begins with a first step."

The interior journey of the soul from the wilds of sin into the enjoyed Presence of God is beautifully illustrated in the Old Testament tabernacle. The returning sinner first entered the outer court where he offered a blood sacrifice on the brazen altar and washed himself in the laver that stood near it. Then through a veil he passed into the holy place where no natural light could come, but the golden candlestick which spoke of Jesus the Light of the World threw its soft glow over all. There also was the shewbread to tell of Jesus, the Bread of Life, and the altar of incense, a figure of unceasing prayer.

Though the worshipper had enjoyed so much, still he had not yet entered the Presence of God. Another veil separated from the Holy of Holies where above the mercy seat dwelt the very God Himself in awful and glorious manifestation. While the tabernacle stood, only the high priest could enter there, and that but once a year, with blood which he offered for his sins and the sins of the people. It was this last veil which was rent when our Lord gave up the ghost on Calvary, and the sacred writer explains that this rending of the veil opened the way for every worshipper in the world to come by the new and living way straight into the divine Presence.

Everything in the New Testament accords with this Old Testament picture. Ransomed men need no longer pause in fear to enter the Holy of Holies. *God wills that we should push on into His Presence and live our whole life there.* This is to be known to us in conscious experience. It is more than a doctrine to be held, it is a life to be enjoyed every moment of every day.

This Flame of the Presence was the beating heart of the Levitical order. Without it all the appointments of the tabernacle were characters of some unknown language; they had no meaning for Israel or for us. The greatest fact of the tabernacle was that *Jehovah was there*; a Presence was waiting within the veil. Similarly the Presence of God is the central fact of Christianity. At the heart of the Christian message is God Himself waiting for His redeemed children to push in to conscious awareness of His Presence. That type of Christianity which happens now to be the vogue knows this Presence only in theory. It fails to stress the Christian's privilege of present realization. According to its teachings we are in the Presence of God positionally, and nothing is said about the need to experience that Presence actually. The fiery urge that drove men like McCheyne is wholly missing. And the present generation of Christians measures itself by this imperfect rule. Ignoble contentment takes the place of burning zeal. We are satisfied to rest in our *judicial* possessions and for the most part we bother ourselves very little about the absence of personal experience.

Who is this within the veil who dwells in fiery manifestations? It is none other than God Himself, "One God the Father Almighty, Maker of heaven and earth, and of all things visible and invisible," and "One Lord Jesus Christ, the only begotten Son of God; begotten of His Father before all worlds, God of God, Light of Light, Very God of Very God; begotten, not made; being of one substance with the Father," and "the Holy Ghost, the Lord and Giver of life, Who proceedeth from the Father and the Son, Who with the Father and the Son together is worshipped and glorified." Yet this holy Trinity is One God, for "we worship one God in Trinity, and Trinity in Unity; neither confounding the Persons, nor dividing the Substance. For there is one Person of the Father, another of the Son, and another of the Holy Ghost. But the Godhead of the Father, of the Son, and of the Holy Ghost, is all one: the glory equal and the majesty co-eternal." So in part run the ancient creeds, and so the inspired Word declares.

Behind the veil is God, that God after Whom the world, with strange inconsistency, has felt, "if haply they might find Him." He has discovered Himself to some extent in nature, but more perfectly in the Incarnation; now He waits to show Himself in ravishing fulness to the humble of soul and the pure in heart.

The world is perishing for lack of the knowledge of God and the Church is famishing for want of His Presence. The instant cure of most of our religious ills would be to enter the Presence in spiritual experience, to become suddenly aware that we are in God and that God is in us. This would lift us out of our pitiful narrowness and cause our hearts to be enlarged. This would burn away the impurities from our lives as the bugs and fungi were burned away by the fire that dwelt in the bush.

What a broad world to roam in, what a sea to swim in is this God and Father of our Lord Jesus Christ. He is *eternal*, which means that He antedates time and is wholly independent of it. Time began in Him and will end in Him. To it He pays no tribute and from it He suffers no change. He is *immutable*, which means that He has never changed and can never change in any smallest measure. To change He would need to go from better to worse or from worse to better. He cannot do either, for being perfect He cannot become more perfect, and if He were to become less perfect He would be less than God. He is *omniscient*, which means that He knows in one free and effortless act all matter, all spirit, all relationships, all events. He has no past and He has no future. He *is*, and none of the limiting and qualifying terms used of creatures can apply to Him. *Love* and *mercy* and *righteousness* are His, and *holiness* so ineffable that no comparisons or figures will avail to express it. Only *fire* can give even a remote conception of it. In fire He appeared at the burning bush; in the pillar of fire He dwelt through all the long wilderness journey. The fire that glowed between the wings of the cherubim in the holy place was called the "shekinah," the Presence, through the years of Israel's glory, and when the Old had given place to the New, He came at Pentecost as a fiery flame and rested upon each disciple.

Spinoza wrote of the intellectual love of God, and he had a measure of truth there; but the highest love of God is not intellectual, it is spiritual. God is spirit and only the spirit of man can know Him really. In the deep spirit of a man the fire must glow or his love is not the true love of God. The great of the Kingdom have been those who loved God more than others did. We all know who they have been and gladly pay tribute to the depths and sincerity of their devotion. We have but to pause for a moment and their names come trooping past us smelling of myrrh and aloes and cassia out of the ivory palaces.

Frederick Faber was one whose soul panted after God as the roe pants after the water brook, and the measure in which God revealed Himself to his seeking heart set the good man's whole life afire with a burning adoration rivaling that of the seraphim before the throne. His love for God extended to the three Persons of the Godhead equally, yet he seemed to feel for each One a special kind of love reserved for Him alone. Of God the Father he sings:

> *Only to sit and think of God,*
> *Oh what a joy it is!*
> *To think the thought, to breathe the Name;*
> *Earth has no higher bliss.*
> *Father of Jesus, love's reward!*
> *What rapture will it be,*
> *Prostrate before Thy throne to lie,*
> *And gaze and gaze on Thee!*

His love for the Person of Christ was so intense that it threatened to consume him; it burned within him as a sweet and holy madness and flowed from his lips like molten gold. In one of his sermons he says, "Wherever we turn in the church of God, there is Jesus. He is the beginning, middle and end of everything to us.... There is nothing good, nothing holy, nothing beautiful, nothing joyous which He is not to His servants. No one need be poor, because, if he chooses, he can have Jesus for his own property and possession. No one need be downcast, for Jesus is the joy of heaven, and it is His joy to enter into sorrowful hearts. We can exaggerate about many things; but we can never exaggerate our obligation to Jesus, or the compassionate abundance of the love of Jesus to us. All our lives long we might talk of Jesus, and yet we should never come to an end of the sweet things that might be said of Him. Eternity will not be long enough to learn all He is, or to praise Him for all He has done, but then, that matters not; for we shall be always with Him, and we desire nothing more." And addressing our Lord directly he says to Him:

> *I love Thee so, I know not how*
> *My transports to control;*
> *Thy love is like a burning fire*
> *Within my very soul.*

Faber's blazing love extended also to the Holy Spirit. Not only in his theology did he acknowledge His deity and full equality with the Father and the Son, but he celebrated it constantly in his songs and in his prayers. He literally pressed his forehead to the ground in his eager fervid worship of the Third Person of the Godhead. In one of his great hymns to the Holy Spirit he sums up his burning devotion thus:

> *O Spirit, beautiful and dread!*
> *My heart is fit to break*
> *With love of all Thy tenderness*
> *For us poor sinners' sake.*

I have risked the tedium of quotation that I might show by pointed example what I have set out to say, viz., that God is so vastly wonderful, so utterly and completely delightful that He can, without anything other than Himself, meet and overflow the deepest demands of our total nature, mysterious and deep as that nature is. Such worship as Faber knew (and he is but one of a great company which no man can number) can never come from a mere doctrinal knowledge of God. Hearts that are "fit to break" with love for the Godhead are those who have been in the Presence and have looked with opened eye upon the majesty of Deity. Men of the breaking hearts had a quality about them not known to or understood by common men. They habitually spoke with spiritual authority. They had been in the Presence of God and they reported what they saw there. They were prophets, not scribes, for the scribe tells us what he has read, and the prophet tells what he has seen.

The distinction is not an imaginary one. Between the scribe who has read and the prophet who has seen there is a difference as wide as the sea. We are today overrun with orthodox scribes, but the prophets, where are they? The hard voice of the scribe sounds over evangelicalism, but the Church waits for the tender voice of the saint who has penetrated the veil and has gazed with inward eye upon the Wonder that is God. And yet, thus to penetrate, to push in sensitive living experience into the holy Presence, is a privilege open to every child of God.

With the veil removed by the rending of Jesus' flesh, with nothing on God's side to prevent us from entering, why do we tarry without? Why do we consent to abide all our days just outside the Holy of Holies and never enter at all to look upon God? We hear the Bridegroom say, "Let me see thy countenance, let me hear thy voice; for sweet is thy voice and thy countenance is comely." We sense that the call is for us, but still we fail to draw near, and the years pass and we grow old and tired in the outer courts of the tabernacle. What doth hinder us?

The answer usually given, simply that we are "cold," will not explain all the facts. There is something more serious than coldness of heart, something that may be back of that coldness and be the cause of its existence. What is it? What but the presence of *a veil in our hearts*? a veil not taken away as the first veil was, but which remains there still shutting out the light and hiding the face of God from us. It is the veil of our fleshly fallen nature living on, unjudged within us, uncrucified and unrepudiated. It is the close-woven veil of the self-life which we have never truly acknowledged, of which we have been secretly ashamed, and which for these reasons we have never brought to the judgment of the cross. It is not too mysterious, this opaque veil, nor is it hard to identify. We have but to look in our own hearts and we shall see it there, sewn and patched and repaired it may be, but there nevertheless, an enemy to our lives and an effective block to our spiritual progress.

This veil is not a beautiful thing and it is not a thing about which we commonly care to talk, but I am addressing the thirsting souls who are determined to follow God, and I know they will not turn back because the way leads temporarily through the blackened hills. The urge of God within them will assure their continuing the pursuit. They will face the facts however unpleasant and endure the cross for the joy set before them. So I am bold to name the threads out of which this inner veil is woven.

It is woven of the fine threads of the self-life, the hyphenated sins of the human spirit. They are not something we do, they are something we *are*, and therein lies both their subtlety and their power.

To be specific, the self-sins are these: self-righteousness, self-pity, self-confidence, self-sufficiency, self-admiration, self-love and a host of others like them. They dwell too deep within us and are too much a part of our natures to come to our attention till the light of God is focused upon them. The grosser manifestations of these sins, egotism, exhibitionism, self-promotion, are strangely tolerated in Christian leaders even in circles of impeccable orthodoxy. They are so much in evidence as actually, for many people, to become identified with the gospel. I trust it is not a cynical observation to say that they appear these days to be a requisite for popularity in some sections of the Church visible. Promoting self under the guise of promoting Christ is currently so common as to excite little notice.

One should suppose that proper instruction in the doctrines of man's depravity and the necessity for justification through the righteousness of Christ alone would deliver us from the power of the self-sins; but it does not work out that way. Self can live unrebuked at the very altar. It can watch the bleeding Victim die and not be in the least affected by what it sees. It can fight for the faith of the Reformers and preach eloquently the creed of salvation by grace, and gain strength by its efforts. To tell all the truth, it seems actually to feed upon orthodoxy and is more at home in a Bible Conference than in a tavern. Our very state of longing after God may afford it an excellent condition under which to thrive and grow.

Self is the opaque veil that hides the Face of God from us. It can be removed only in spiritual experience, never by mere instruction. As well try to instruct leprosy out of our system. There must be a work of God in destruction before we are free. We must invite the cross to do its deadly work within us. We must bring our self-sins to the cross for judgment. We must prepare ourselves for an ordeal of suffering in some measure like that through which our Saviour passed when He suffered under Pontius Pilate.

Let us remember: when we talk of the rending of the veil we are speaking in a figure, and the thought of it is poetical, almost pleasant; but in actuality there is nothing pleasant about it. In human experience that veil is made of living spiritual tissue; it is composed of the sentient, quivering stuff of which our whole beings consist, and to touch it is to touch us where we feel pain. To tear it away is to injure us, to hurt us and make us bleed. To say otherwise is to make the cross no cross and death no death at all. It is never fun to die. To rip through the dear and tender stuff of which life is made can never be anything but deeply painful. Yet that is what the cross did to Jesus and it is what the cross would do to every man to set him free.

Let us beware of tinkering with our inner life in hope ourselves to rend the veil. God must do everything for us. Our part is to yield and trust. We must confess, forsake, repudiate the self-life, and then reckon it crucified. But we must be careful to distinguish lazy "acceptance" from the real work of God. We must insist upon the work being done. We dare not rest content with a neat doctrine of self-crucifixion. That is to imitate Saul and spare the best of the sheep and the oxen.

Insist that the work be done in very truth and it will be done. The cross is rough, and it is deadly, but it is effective. It does not keep its victim hanging there forever. There comes a moment when its work is finished and the suffering victim dies. After that is resurrection glory and power, and the pain is forgotten for joy that the veil is taken away and we have entered in actual spiritual experience the Presence of the living God.

*　　*　　*

Lord, how excellent are Thy ways, and how devious and dark are the ways of man. Show us how to die, that we may rise again to newness of life. Rend the veil of our self-life from the top down as Thou didst rend the veil of the Temple. We would draw near in full assurance of faith. We would dwell with Thee in daily experience here on this earth so that we may be accustomed to the glory when we enter Thy heaven to dwell with Thee there.

In Jesus' name, Amen.

4
APPREHENDING GOD

O taste and see.—Psa. 34:8

It was Canon Holmes, of India, who more than twenty-five years ago called attention to the inferential character of the average man's faith in God. To most people God is an inference, not a reality. He is a deduction from evidence which they consider adequate; but He remains personally unknown to the individual. "He *must* be," they say, "therefore we believe He is." Others do not go even so far as this; they know of Him only by hearsay. They have never bothered to think the matter out for themselves, but have heard about Him from others, and have put belief in Him into the back of their minds along with the various odds and ends that make up their total creed. To many others God is but an ideal, another name for goodness, or beauty, or truth; or He is law, or life, or the creative impulse back of the phenomena of existence.

These notions about God are many and varied, but they who hold them have one thing in common: they do not know God in personal experience. The possibility of intimate acquaintance with Him has not entered their minds. While admitting His existence they do not think of Him as knowable in the sense that we know things or people.

Christians, to be sure, go further than this, at least in theory. Their creed requires them to believe in the personality of God, and they have been taught to pray, "Our Father, which art in heaven." Now personality and fatherhood carry with them the idea of the possibility of personal acquaintance. This is admitted, I say, in theory, but for millions of Christians, nevertheless, God is no more real than He is to the non-Christian. They go through life trying to love an ideal and be loyal to a mere principle.

Over against all this cloudy vagueness stands the clear scriptural doctrine that God can be known in personal experience. A loving Personality dominates the Bible, walking among the trees of the garden and breathing fragrance over every scene. Always a living Person is present, speaking, pleading, loving, working, and manifesting Himself whenever and wherever His people have the receptivity necessary to receive the manifestation.

The Bible assumes as a self-evident fact that men can know God with at least the same degree of immediacy as they know any other person or thing that comes within the field of their experience. The same terms are used to express the knowledge of God as are used to express knowledge of physical things. "O *taste* and see that the Lord is good." "All thy garments *smell* of myrrh, and aloes, and cassia, out of the ivory palaces." "My sheep *hear* my voice." "Blessed are the pure in heart, for they shall *see* God." These are but four of countless such passages from the Word of God. And more important than any proof text is the fact that the whole import of the Scripture is toward this belief.

What can all this mean except that we have in our hearts organs by means of which we can know God as certainly as we know material things through our familiar five senses? We apprehend the physical world by exercising the faculties given us for the purpose, and we possess spiritual faculties by means of which we can know God and the spiritual world if we will obey the Spirit's urge and begin to use them.

That a saving work must first be done in the heart is taken for granted here. The spiritual faculties of the unregenerate man lie asleep in his nature, unused and for every purpose dead; that is the stroke which has fallen upon us by sin. They may be quickened to active life again by the operation of the Holy Spirit in regeneration; that is one of the immeasurable benefits which come to us through Christ's atoning work on the cross.

But the very ransomed children of God themselves: why do they know so little of that habitual conscious communion with God which the Scriptures seem to offer? The answer is our chronic unbelief. Faith enables our spiritual sense to function. Where faith is defective the result will be inward insensibility and numbness toward spiritual things. This is the condition of vast numbers of Christians today. No proof is necessary to support that statement. We have but to converse with the first Christian we meet or enter the first church we find open to acquire all the proof we need.

A spiritual kingdom lies all about us, enclosing us, embracing us, altogether within reach of our inner selves, waiting for us to recognize it. God Himself is here waiting our response to His Presence. This eternal world will come alive to us the moment we begin to reckon upon its reality.

I have just now used two words which demand definition; or if definition is impossible, I must at least make clear what I mean when I use them. They are "reckon" and "reality."

What do I mean by *reality*? I mean that which has existence apart from any idea any mind may have of it, and which would exist if there were no mind anywhere to entertain a thought of it. That which is real has being in itself. It does not depend upon the observer for its validity.

I am aware that there are those who love to poke fun at the plain man's idea of reality. They are the idealists who spin endless proofs that nothing is real outside of the mind. They are the relativists who like to show that there are no fixed points in the universe from which we can measure anything. They smile down upon us from their lofty intellectual peaks and settle us to their own satisfaction by fastening upon us the reproachful term "absolutist." The Christian is not put out of countenance by this show of contempt. He can smile right back at them, for he knows that there is only One who is Absolute, that is God. But he knows also that the Absolute One has made this world for man's uses, and, while there is nothing fixed or real in the last meaning of the words (the meaning as applied to God) *for every purpose of human life we are permitted to act as if there were.* And every man does act thus except the mentally sick. These unfortunates also have trouble with reality, but they are consistent; they insist upon living in accordance with their ideas of things. They are honest, and it is their very honesty that constitutes them a social problem.

The idealists and relativists are not mentally sick. They prove their soundness by living their lives according to the very notions of reality which they in theory repudiate and by counting upon the very fixed points which they prove are not there. They could earn a lot more respect for their notions if they were willing to live by them; but this they are careful not to do. Their ideas are brain-deep, not life-deep. Wherever life touches them they repudiate their theories and live like other men.

The Christian is too sincere to play with ideas for their own sake. He takes no pleasure in the mere spinning of gossamer webs for display. All his beliefs are practical. They are geared into his life. By them he lives or dies, stands or falls for this world and for all time to come. From the insincere man he turns away.

The sincere plain man knows that the world is real. He finds it here when he wakes to consciousness, and he knows that he did not think it into being. It was here waiting for him when he came, and he knows that when he prepares to leave this earthly scene it will be here still to bid him good-bye as he departs. By the deep wisdom of life he is wiser than a thousand men who doubt. He stands upon the earth and feels the wind and rain in his face and he knows that they are real. He sees the sun by day and the stars by night. He sees the hot lightning play out of the dark thundercloud. He hears the sounds of nature and the cries of human joy and pain. These he knows are real. He lies down on the cool earth at night and has no fear that it will prove illusory or fail him while he sleeps. In the morning the firm ground will be under him, the blue sky above him and the rocks and trees around him as when he closed his eyes the night before. So he lives and rejoices in a world of reality.

With his five senses he engages this real world. All things necessary to his physical existence he apprehends by the faculties with which he has been equipped by the God who created him and placed him in such a world as this.

Now, by our definition also God is real. He is real in the absolute and final sense that nothing else is. All other reality is contingent upon His. The great Reality is God who is the Author of that lower and dependent reality which makes up the sum of created things, including ourselves. God has objective existence independent of and apart from any notions which we may have concerning Him. The worshipping heart does not create its Object. It finds Him here when it wakes from its moral slumber in the morning of its regeneration.

Another word that must be cleared up is the word *reckon*. This does not mean to visualize or imagine. Imagination is not faith. The two are not only different from, but stand in sharp opposition to, each other. Imagination projects unreal images out of the mind and seeks to attach reality to them. Faith creates nothing; it simply reckons upon that which is already *there*.

God and the spiritual world are real. We can reckon upon them with as much assurance as we reckon upon the familiar world around us. Spiritual things are there (or rather we should say *here*) inviting our attention and challenging our trust.

Our trouble is that we have established bad thought habits. We habitually think of the visible world as real and doubt the reality of any other. We do not deny the existence of the spiritual world but we doubt that it is real in the accepted meaning of the word.

The world of sense intrudes upon our attention day and night for the whole of our lifetime. It is clamorous, insistent and self-demonstrating. It does not appeal to our faith; it is here, assaulting our five senses, demanding to be accepted as real and final. But sin has so clouded the lenses of our hearts that we cannot see that other reality, the City of God, shining around us. The world of sense triumphs. The visible becomes the enemy of the invisible; the temporal, of the eternal. That is the curse inherited by every member of Adam's tragic race.

At the root of the Christian life lies belief in the invisible. The object of the Christian's faith is unseen reality.

Our uncorrected thinking, influenced by the blindness of our natural hearts and the intrusive ubiquity of visible things, tends to draw a contrast between the spiritual and the real; but actually no such contrast exists. The antithesis lies elsewhere: between the real and the imaginary, between the spiritual and the material, between the temporal and the eternal; but between the spiritual and the real, never. The spiritual *is* real.

If we would rise into that region of light and power plainly beckoning us through the Scriptures of truth we must break the evil habit of ignoring the spiritual. We must shift our interest from the seen to the unseen. For the great unseen Reality is God. "He that cometh to God must believe that he is, and that he is a rewarder of them that diligently seek him." This is basic in the life of faith. From there we can rise to unlimited heights. "Ye believe in God," said our Lord Jesus Christ, "believe also in me." Without the first there can be no second.

If we truly want to follow God we must seek to be other-worldly. This I say knowing well that that word has been used with scorn by the sons of this world and applied to the Christian as a badge of reproach. So be it. Every man must choose his world. If we who follow Christ, with all the facts before us and knowing what we are about, deliberately choose the Kingdom of God as our sphere of interest I see no reason why anyone should object. If we lose by it, the loss is our own; if we gain, we rob no one by so doing. The "other world," which is the object of this world's disdain and the subject of the drunkard's mocking song, is our carefully chosen goal and the object of our holiest longing.

But we must avoid the common fault of pushing the "other world" into the future. It is not future, but present. It parallels our familiar physical world, and the doors between the two worlds are open. "Ye are come," says the writer to the Hebrews (and the tense is plainly present), "unto Mount Zion, and unto the city of the living God, the heavenly Jerusalem, and to an innumerable company of angels, to the general assembly and church of the firstborn, which are written in heaven, and to God the Judge of all, and to the spirits of just men made perfect, and to Jesus the mediator of the new covenant, and to the blood of sprinkling, that speaketh better things than that of Abel." All these things are contrasted with "the mount that might be touched" and "the sound of a trumpet and the voice of words" that might be heard. May we not safely conclude that, as the realities of Mount Sinai were apprehended by the senses, so the realities of Mount Zion are to be grasped by the soul? And this not by any trick of the imagination, but in downright actuality. The soul has eyes with which to see and ears with which to hear. Feeble they may be from long disuse, but by the life-giving touch of Christ alive now and capable of sharpest sight and most sensitive hearing.

As we begin to focus upon God the things of the spirit will take shape before our inner eyes. Obedience to the word of Christ will bring an inward revelation of the Godhead (John 14:21-23). It will give acute perception enabling us to see God even as is promised to the pure in heart. A new God consciousness will seize upon us and we shall begin to taste and hear and inwardly feel the God who is our life and our all. There will be seen the constant shining of the light that lighteth every man that cometh into the world. More and more, as our faculties grow sharper and more sure, God will become to us the great All, and His Presence the glory and wonder of our lives.

*   *   *

O God, quicken to life every power within me, that I may lay hold on eternal things. Open my eyes that I may see; give me acute spiritual perception; enable me to taste

Thee and know that Thou art good. Make heaven more
real to me than any earthly thing has ever been.

Amen.

5
THE UNIVERSAL PRESENCE

Whither shall I go from thy spirit? or whither shall I flee from thy presence?—Psa. 139:7

In all Christian teaching certain basic truths are found, hidden at times, and rather assumed than asserted, but necessary to all truth as the primary colors are found in and necessary to the finished painting. Such a truth is the divine immanence.

God dwells in His creation and is everywhere indivisibly present in all His works. This is boldly taught by prophet and apostle and is accepted by Christian theology generally. That is, it appears in the books, but for some reason it has not sunk into the average Christian's heart so as to become a part of his believing self. Christian teachers shy away from its full implications, and, if they mention it at all, mute it down till it has little meaning. I would guess the reason for this to be the fear of being charged with pantheism; but the doctrine of the divine Presence is definitely not pantheism.

Pantheism's error is too palpable to deceive anyone. It is that God is the sum of all created things. Nature and God are one, so that whoever touches a leaf or a stone touches God. That is of course to degrade the glory of the incorruptible Deity and, in an effort to make all things divine, banish all divinity from the world entirely.

The truth is that while God dwells in His world He is separated from it by a gulf forever impassable. However closely He may be identified with the work of His hands *they* are and must eternally be *other than He*, and He is and must be antecedent to and independent of them. He is transcendent above all His works even while He is immanent within them.

What now does the divine immanence mean in direct Christian experience? It means simply that *God is here*. Wherever we are, God is here. There is no place, there can be no place, where He is not. Ten million intelligences standing at as many points in space and separated by incomprehensible distances can each one say with equal truth, God is here. No point is nearer to God than any other point. It is exactly as near to God from any place as it is from any other place. No one is in mere distance any further from or any nearer to God than any other person is.

These are truths believed by every instructed Christian. It remains for us to think on them and pray over them until they begin to glow within us.

"In the beginning God." Not *matter*, for matter is not self-causing. It requires an antecedent cause, and God is that Cause. Not *law*, for law is but a name for the course which all creation follows. That course had to be planned, and the Planner is God. Not *mind*, for mind also is a created thing and must have a Creator back of it. In the beginning God, the uncaused Cause of matter, mind and law. There we must begin.

Adam sinned and, in his panic, frantically tried to do the impossible: he tried to hide from the Presence of God. David also must have had wild thoughts of trying to escape from the Presence, for he wrote, "Whither shall I go from thy spirit? or whither shall I flee from thy presence?" Then he proceeded through one of his most beautiful psalms to celebrate the glory of the divine immanence. "If I ascend up into heaven, thou art there: if I make my bed in hell, behold, thou art there. If I take the wings of the morning, and dwell in the uttermost parts of the sea; even there shall thy hand lead me, and thy right hand shall hold me." And he knew that God's *being* and God's *seeing* are the same, that the seeing Presence had been with him even before he was born, watching the mystery of unfolding life. Solomon exclaimed, "But will God indeed dwell on the earth? behold the heaven and the heaven of heavens cannot contain thee: how much less this house which I have builded." Paul assured the Athenians that "God is not far from any one of us: for in him we live, and move, and have our being."

If God is present at every point in space, if we cannot go where He is not, cannot even conceive of a place where He is not, why then has not that Presence become the one universally celebrated fact of the world? The patriarch Jacob, "in the waste howling wilderness," gave the answer to that question. He saw a vision of God and cried out in wonder, "Surely the Lord is in this place; and I knew it not." Jacob had never been for one small division of a moment outside the circle of that all-pervading Presence. But he knew it not. That was his trouble, and it is ours. Men do not know that God is here. What a difference it would make if they knew.

The Presence and the manifestation of the Presence are not the same. There can be the one without the other. God is here when we are wholly unaware of it. He is *manifest* only when and as we are aware of His Presence. On our part there must be surrender to the Spirit of God, for His work it is to show us the Father and the Son. If we co-operate with Him in loving obedience God will manifest Himself to us, and that manifestation will be the difference between a nominal Christian life and a life radiant with the light of His face.

Always, everywhere God is present, and always He seeks to discover Himself. To each one he would reveal not only that He is, but *what* He is as well. He did not have to be persuaded to discover Himself to Moses. "And the Lord descended in the cloud, and stood with him there, and proclaimed the name of the Lord." He not only made a verbal proclamation of His nature but He revealed His very Self to Moses so that the skin of Moses' face shone with the supernatural light. It will be a great moment for some of us when we begin to believe that God's promise of self-revelation is literally true: that He promised much, but promised no more than He intends to fulfill.

Our pursuit of God is successful just because He is forever seeking to manifest Himself to us. The revelation of God to any man is not God coming from a distance upon a time to pay a brief and momentous visit to the man's soul. Thus to think of it is to misunderstand it all. The approach of God to the soul or of the soul to God is not to be thought of in spatial terms at all. There is no idea of physical distance involved in the concept. It is not a matter of miles but of experience.

To speak of being near to or far from God is to use language in a sense always understood when applied to our ordinary human relationships. A man may say, "I feel that my son is coming nearer to me as he gets older," and yet that son has lived by his father's side since he was born and has never been away from home more than a day or so in his entire life. What then can the father mean? Obviously he is speaking of *experience*. He means that the boy is coming to know him more intimately and with deeper understanding, that the barriers of thought and feeling between the two are disappearing, that father and son are becoming more closely united in mind and heart.

So when we sing, "Draw me nearer, nearer, blessed Lord," we are not thinking of the nearness of place, but of the nearness of relationship. It is for increasing degrees of awareness that we pray, for a more perfect consciousness of the divine Presence. We need never shout across the spaces to an absent God. He is nearer than our own soul, closer than our most secret thoughts.

Why do some persons "find" God in a way that others do not? Why does God manifest His Presence to some and let multitudes of others struggle along in the half-light of imperfect Christian experience? Of course the will of God is the same for all. He has no favorites within His household. All He has ever done for any of His children He will do for all of His children. The difference lies not with God but with us.

Pick at random a score of great saints whose lives and testimonies are widely known. Let them be Bible characters or well known Christians of post-Biblical times. You will be struck instantly with the fact that the saints were not alike. Sometimes the unlikenesses were so great as to be positively glaring. How different for example was Moses from Isaiah; how different was Elijah from David; how unlike each other were John and Paul, St. Francis and Luther, Finney and Thomas à Kempis. The differences are as wide as human life itself: differences of race, nationality, education, temperament, habit and personal qualities. Yet they all walked, each in his day, upon a high road of spiritual living far above the common way.

Their differences must have been incidental and in the eyes of God of no significance. In some vital quality they must have been alike. What was it?

I venture to suggest that the one vital quality which they had in common was *spiritual receptivity*. Something in them was open to heaven, something which urged them Godward. Without attempting anything like a profound analysis I shall say simply that they had spiritual awareness and that they went on to cultivate it until it became the biggest thing in their lives. They differed from the average person in that when they felt the inward longing they *did something about it*. They acquired the lifelong habit of spiritual response. They were not disobedient to the heavenly vision. As David put it neatly, "When thou saidst, Seek ye my face; my heart said unto thee, Thy face, Lord, will I seek."

As with everything good in human life, back of this receptivity is God. The sovereignty of God is here, and is felt even by those who have not placed particular stress upon it theologically. The pious Michael Angelo confessed this in a sonnet:

> *My unassisted heart is barren clay,*
> *That of its native self can nothing feed:*
> *Of good and pious works Thou art the seed,*
> *That quickens only where Thou sayest it may:*
> *Unless Thou show to us Thine own true way*
> *No man can find it: Father! Thou must lead.*

These words will repay study as the deep and serious testimony of a great Christian.

Important as it is that we recognize God working in us, I would yet warn against a too-great preoccupation with the thought. It is a sure road to sterile passivity. God will not hold us responsible to understand the mysteries of election, predestination and the divine sovereignty. The best and safest way to deal with these truths is to raise our eyes to God and in deepest reverence say, "O Lord, Thou knowest." Those things belong to the deep and mysterious Profound of God's omniscience. Prying into them may make theologians, but it will never make saints.

Receptivity is not a single thing; it is a compound rather, a blending of several elements within the soul. It is an affinity for, a bent toward, a sympathetic response to, a desire to have. From this it may be gathered that it can be present in degrees, that we may have little or more or less, depending upon the individual. It may be increased by exercise or destroyed by neglect. It is not a sovereign and irresistible force which comes upon us as a seizure from above. It is a gift of God, indeed, but one which must be recognized and cultivated as any other gift if it is to realize the purpose for which it was given.

Failure to see this is the cause of a very serious breakdown in modern evangelicalism. The idea of cultivation and exercise, so dear to the saints of old, has now no place in our total religious picture. It is too slow, too common. We now demand glamour and fast flowing dramatic action. A generation of Christians reared among push buttons and automatic machines is impatient of slower and less direct methods of reaching their goals. We have been trying to apply machine-age methods to our relations with God. We read our chapter, have our short devotions and rush away, hoping to make up for our deep inward bankruptcy by attending another gospel meeting or listening to another thrilling story told by a religious adventurer lately returned from afar.

The tragic results of this spirit are all about us. Shallow lives, hollow religious philosophies, the preponderance of the element of fun in gospel meetings, the glorification of men, trust in religious externalities, quasi-religious fellowships, salesmanship methods, the mistaking of dynamic personality for the power of the Spirit: these and such as these are the symptoms of an evil disease, a deep and serious malady of the soul.

For this great sickness that is upon us no one person is responsible, and no Christian is wholly free from blame. We have all contributed, directly or indirectly, to this sad state of affairs. We have been too blind to see, or too timid to speak out, or too self-satisfied to desire anything better than the poor average diet with which others appear satisfied. To put it differently, we have accepted one another's notions, copied one another's lives and made one another's experiences the model for our own. And for a generation the trend has been downward. Now we have reached a low place of sand and burnt wire grass and, worst of all, we have made the Word of Truth conform to our experience and accepted this low plane as the very pasture of the blessed.

It will require a determined heart and more than a little courage to wrench ourselves loose from the grip of our times and return to Biblical ways. But it can be done. Every now and then in the past Christians have had to do it. History has recorded several large-scale returns led by such men as St. Francis, Martin Luther and George Fox. Unfortunately there seems to be no Luther or Fox on the horizon at present. Whether or not another such return may be expected before the coming of Christ is a question upon which Christians are not fully agreed, but that is not of too great importance to us now.

What God in His sovereignty may yet do on a world-scale I do not claim to know: but what He will do for the plain man or woman who seeks His face I believe I do know and can tell others. Let any man turn to God in earnest, let him begin to exercise himself unto godliness, let him seek to develop his powers of spiritual receptivity by trust and obedience and humility, and the results will exceed anything he may have hoped in his leaner and weaker days.

Any man who by repentance and a sincere return to God will break himself out of the mold in which he has been held, and will go to the Bible itself for his spiritual standards, will be delighted with what he finds there.

Let us say it again: The Universal Presence is a fact. God is here. The whole universe is alive with His life. And He is no strange or foreign God, but the familiar Father of our Lord Jesus Christ whose love has for these thousands of years enfolded the sinful race of men. And always He is trying to get our attention, to reveal Himself to us, to communicate with us. We have within us the ability to know Him if we will but respond to His overtures. (And this we call pursuing God!) We will know Him in increasing degree as our receptivity becomes more perfect by faith and love and practice.

*   *   *

O God and Father, I repent of my sinful preoccupation with visible things. The world has been too much with me. Thou hast been here and I knew it not. I have been blind to Thy Presence. Open my eyes that I may behold Thee in and around me.

For Christ's sake, Amen.

6
THE SPEAKING VOICE

In the beginning was the Word, and the Word was with God, and the Word was God.—John 1:1

An intelligent plain man, untaught in the truths of Christianity, coming upon this text, would likely conclude that John meant to teach that it is the nature of God to speak, to communicate His thoughts to others. And he would be right. A word is a medium by which thoughts are expressed, and the application of term to the Eternal Son leads us to believe that self-expression is inherent in the Godhead, that God is forever seeking to speak Himself out to His creation. The whole Bible supports the idea. God is speaking. Not God spoke, but *God is speaking*. He is by His nature continuously articulate. He fills the world with His speaking Voice.

One of the great realities with which we have to deal is the Voice of God in His world. The briefest and only satisfying cosmogony is this: "He spake and it was done." The *why* of natural law is the living Voice of God immanent in His creation. And this word of God which brought all worlds into being cannot be understood to mean the Bible, for it is not a written or printed word at all, but the expression of the will of God spoken into the structure of all things. This word of God is the breath of God filling the world with living potentiality. The Voice of God is the most powerful force in nature, indeed the only force in nature, for all energy is here only because the power-filled Word is being spoken.

The Bible is the written word of God, and because it is written it is confined and limited by the necessities of ink and paper and leather. The Voice of God, however, is alive and free as the sovereign God is free.

"The words that I speak unto you, they are spirit, and they are life." The life is in the speaking words. God's word in the Bible can have power only because it corresponds to God's word in the universe. It is the present Voice which makes the written Word all-powerful. Otherwise it would lie locked in slumber within the covers of a book.

We take a low and primitive view of things when we conceive of God at the creation coming into physical contact with things, shaping and fitting and building like a carpenter. The Bible teaches otherwise: "By the word of the Lord were the heavens made; and all the host of them by the breath of his mouth.... For he spake, and it was done; he commanded, and it stood fast." "Through faith we understand that the worlds were framed by the word of God." Again we must remember that God is referring here not to His written Word, but to His speaking Voice. His world-filling Voice is meant, that Voice which antedates the Bible by uncounted centuries, that Voice which has not been silent since the dawn of creation, but is sounding still throughout the full far reaches of the universe.

The Word of God is quick and powerful. In the beginning He spoke to nothing, and it became *something*. Chaos heard it and became order, darkness heard it and became light. "And God said—and it was so." These twin phrases, as cause and effect, occur throughout the Genesis story of the creation. The *said* accounts for the *so*. The *so* is the *said* put into the continuous present.

That God is here and that He is speaking—these truths are back of all other Bible truths; without them there could be no revelation at all. God did not write a book and send it by messenger to be read at a distance by unaided minds. He spoke a Book and lives in His spoken words, constantly speaking His words and causing the power of them to persist across the years. God breathed on clay and it became a man; He breathes on men and they become clay. "Return ye children of men" was the word spoken at the Fall by which God decreed the death of every man, and no added word has He needed to speak. The sad procession of mankind across the face of the earth from birth to the grave is proof that His original Word was enough.

We have not given sufficient attention to that deep utterance in the Book of John, "That was the true Light, which lighteth every man that cometh into the world." Shift the punctuation around as we will and the truth is still there: the Word of God affects the hearts of all men as light in the soul. In the hearts of all men the light shines, the Word sounds, and there is no escaping them. Something like this would of necessity be so if God is alive and in His world. And John says that it is so. Even those persons who have never heard of the Bible have still been preached to with sufficient clarity to remove every excuse from their hearts forever. "Which show the work of the law written in their hearts, their conscience also bearing witness, and their thoughts the mean while either accusing or else excusing one another." "For the invisible things of him from the creation of the world are clearly seen, being understood by the things that are made, even his eternal power and Godhead; so that they are without excuse."

This universal Voice of God was by the ancient Hebrews often called Wisdom, and was said to be everywhere sounding and searching throughout the earth, seeking some response from the sons of men. The eighth chapter of the Book of Proverbs begins, "Doth not wisdom cry? and understanding put forth her voice?" The writer then pictures wisdom as a beautiful woman standing "in the top of the high places, by the way in the places of the paths." She sounds her voice from every quarter so that no one may miss hearing it. "Unto you, O men, I call; and my voice is to the sons of men." Then she pleads for the simple and the foolish to give ear to her words. It is spiritual response for which this Wisdom of God is pleading, a response which she has always sought and is but rarely able to secure. The tragedy is that our eternal welfare depends upon our hearing, and we have trained our ears not to hear.

This universal Voice has ever sounded, and it has often troubled men even when they did not understand the source of their fears. Could it be that this Voice distilling like a living mist upon the hearts of men has been the undiscovered cause of the troubled conscience and the longing for immortality confessed by millions since the dawn of recorded history? We need not fear to face up to this. The speaking Voice is a fact. How men have reacted to it is for any observer to note.

When God spoke out of heaven to our Lord, self-centered men who heard it explained it by natural causes: they said, "It thundered." This habit of explaining the Voice by appeals to natural law is at the very root of modern science. In the living breathing cosmos there is a mysterious Something, too wonderful, too awful for any mind to understand. The believing man does not claim to understand. He falls to his knees and whispers, "God." The man of earth kneels also, but not to worship. He kneels to examine, to search, to find the cause and the how of things. Just now we happen to be living in a secular age. Our thought habits are those of the scientist, not those of the worshipper. We are more likely to explain than to adore. "It thundered," we exclaim, and go our earthly way. But still the Voice sounds and searches. The order and life of the world depend upon that Voice, but men are mostly too busy or too stubborn to give attention.

Everyone of us has had experiences which we have not been able to explain: a sudden sense of loneliness, or a feeling of wonder or awe in the face of the universal vastness. Or we have had a fleeting visitation of light like an illumination from some other sun, giving us in a quick flash an assurance that we are from another world, that our origins are divine. What we saw there, or felt, or heard, may have been contrary to all that we had been taught in the schools and at wide variance with all our former beliefs and opinions. We were forced to suspend our acquired doubts while, for a moment, the clouds were rolled back and we saw and heard for ourselves. Explain such things as we will, I think we have not been fair to the facts until we allow at least the possibility that such experiences may arise from the Presence of God in the world and His persistent effort to communicate with mankind. Let us not dismiss such an hypothesis too flippantly.

It is my own belief (and here I shall not feel bad if no one follows me) that every good and beautiful thing which man has produced in the world has been the result of his faulty and sin-blocked response to the creative Voice sounding over the earth. The moral philosophers who dreamed their high dreams of virtue, the religious thinkers who speculated about God and immortality, the poets and artists who created out of common stuff pure and lasting beauty: how can we explain them? It is not enough to say simply, "It was genius." What then is genius? Could it be that a genius is a man haunted by the speaking Voice, laboring and striving like one possessed to achieve ends which he only vaguely understands? That the great man may have missed God in his labors, that he may even have spoken or written against God does not destroy the idea I am advancing. God's redemptive revelation in the Holy Scriptures is necessary to saving faith and peace with God. Faith in a risen Saviour is necessary if the vague stirrings toward immortality are to bring us to restful and satisfying communion with God. To me this is a plausible explanation of all that is best out of Christ. But you can be a good Christian and not accept my thesis.

The Voice of God is a friendly Voice. No one need fear to listen to it unless he has already made up his mind to resist it. The blood of Jesus has covered not only the human race but all creation as well. "And having made peace through the blood of his cross, by him to reconcile all things unto himself; by him, I say, whether they be things in earth, or things in heaven." We may safely preach a friendly Heaven. The heavens as well as the earth are filled with the good will of Him that dwelt in the bush. The perfect blood of atonement secures this forever.

Whoever will listen will hear the speaking Heaven. This is definitely not the hour when men take kindly to an exhortation to *listen*, for listening is not today a part of popular religion. We are at the opposite end of the pole from there. Religion has accepted the monstrous heresy that noise, size, activity and bluster make a man dear to God. But we may take heart. To a people caught in the tempest of the last great conflict God says, "Be still, and know that I am God," and still He says it, as if He means to tell us that our strength and safety lie not in noise but in silence.

It is important that we get still to wait on God. And it is best that we get alone, preferably with our Bible outspread before us. Then if we will we may draw near to God and begin to hear Him speak to us in our hearts. I think for the average person the progression will be something like this: First a sound as of a Presence walking in the garden. Then a voice, more intelligible, but still far from clear. Then the happy moment when the Spirit begins to illuminate the Scriptures, and that which had been only a sound, or at best a voice, now becomes an intelligible word, warm and intimate and clear as the word of a dear friend. Then will come life and light, and best of all, ability to see and rest in and embrace Jesus Christ as Saviour and Lord and All.

The Bible will never be a living Book to us until we are convinced that God is articulate in His universe. To jump from a dead, impersonal world to a dogmatic Bible is too much for most people. They may admit that they *should* accept the Bible as the Word of God, and they may try to think of it as such, but they find it impossible to believe that the words there on the page are actually for them. A man may *say*, "These words are addressed to me," and yet in his heart not feel and know that they are. He is the victim of a divided psychology. He tries to think of God as mute everywhere else and vocal only in a book.

I believe that much of our religious unbelief is due to a wrong conception of and a wrong feeling for the Scriptures of Truth. A silent God suddenly began to speak in a book and when the book was finished lapsed back into silence again forever. Now we read the book as the record of what God said when He was for a brief time in a speaking mood. With notions like that in our heads how can we believe? The facts are that God is not silent, has never been silent. It is the nature of God to speak. The second Person of the Holy Trinity is called the *Word*. The Bible is the inevitable outcome of God's continuous speech. It is the infallible declaration of His mind for us put into our familiar human words.

I think a new world will arise out of the religious mists when we approach our Bible with the idea that it is not only a book which was once spoken, but a book which is *now speaking*. The prophets habitually said, "Thus *saith* the Lord." They meant their hearers to understand that God's speaking is in the continuous present. We may use the past tense properly to indicate that at a certain time a certain word of God was spoken, but a word of God once spoken continues to be spoken, as a child once born continues to be alive, or a world once created continues to exist. And those are but imperfect illustrations, for children die and worlds burn out, but the Word of our God endureth forever.

If you would follow on to know the Lord, come at once to the open Bible expecting it to speak to you. Do not come with the notion that it is a *thing* which you may push around at your convenience. It is more than a thing, it is a voice, a word, the very Word of the living God.

*   *   *

Lord, teach me to listen. The times are noisy and my ears are weary with the thousand raucous sounds which continuously assault them. Give me the spirit of the boy Samuel when he said to Thee, "Speak, for thy servant heareth." Let me hear Thee speaking in my heart. Let me get used to the sound of Thy Voice, that its tones may be familiar when the sounds of earth die away and the only sound will be the music of Thy speaking Voice.

Amen.

7
THE GAZE OF THE SOUL

***Looking unto Jesus the author and finisher of our
faith.***—Heb. 12:2

L et us think of our intelligent plain man mentioned in chapter six
coming for the first time to the reading of the Scriptures. He approaches the Bible without any previous knowledge of what it contains.
He is wholly without prejudice; he has nothing to prove and nothing to
defend.

Such a man will not have read long until his mind begins to observe
certain truths standing out from the page. They are the spiritual principles behind the record of God's dealings with men, and woven into the
writings of holy men as they "were moved by the Holy Ghost." As he
reads on he might want to number these truths as they become clear to
him and make a brief summary under each number. These summaries
will be the tenets of his Biblical creed. Further reading will not affect
these points except to enlarge and strengthen them. Our man is finding
out what the Bible actually teaches.

High up on the list of things which the Bible teaches will be the doctrine of *faith*. The place of weighty importance which the Bible gives
to faith will be too plain for him to miss. He will very likely conclude:
Faith is all-important in the life of the soul. Without faith it is impossible to please God. Faith will get me anything, take me anywhere in the
Kingdom of God, but without faith there can be no approach to God, no
forgiveness, no deliverance, no salvation, no communion, no spiritual
life at all.

By the time our friend has reached the eleventh chapter of Hebrews the eloquent encomium which is there pronounced upon faith will not seem strange to him. He will have read Paul's powerful defense of faith in his Roman and Galatian epistles. Later if he goes on to study church history he will understand the amazing power in the teachings of the Reformers as they showed the central place of faith in the Christian religion.

Now if faith is so vitally important, if it is an indispensable *must* in our pursuit of God, it is perfectly natural that we should be deeply concerned over whether or not we possess this most precious gift. And our minds being what they are, it is inevitable that sooner or later we should get around to inquiring after the nature of faith. What *is* faith? would lie close to the question, Do I *have* faith? and would demand an answer if it were anywhere to be found.

Almost all who preach or write on the subject of faith have much the same things to say concerning it. They tell us that it is believing a promise, that it is taking God at His word, that it is reckoning the Bible to be true and stepping out upon it. The rest of the book or sermon is usually taken up with stories of persons who have had their prayers answered as a result of their faith. These answers are mostly direct gifts of a practical and temporal nature such as health, money, physical protection or success in business. Or if the teacher is of a philosophic turn of mind he may take another course and lose us in a welter of metaphysics or snow us under with psychological jargon as he defines and re-defines, paring the slender hair of faith thinner and thinner till it disappears in gossamer shavings at last. When he is finished we get up disappointed and go out "by that same door where in we went." Surely there must be something better than this.

In the Scriptures there is practically no effort made to define faith. Outside of a brief fourteen-word definition in Hebrews 11:1, I know of no Biblical definition, and even there faith is defined functionally, not philosophically; that is, it is a statement of what faith is *in operation, not* what it is *in essence*. It assumes the presence of faith and shows what it results in, rather than what it is. We will be wise to go just that far and attempt to go no further. We are told from whence it comes and by what means: "Faith is a gift of God," and "Faith cometh by hearing, and hearing by the word of God." This much is clear, and, to paraphrase Thomas à Kempis, "I had rather exercise faith than know the definition thereof."

From here on, when the words "faith is" or their equivalent occur in

this chapter I ask that they be understood to refer to what faith is in operation as exercised by a believing man. Right here we drop the notion of
definition and think about faith as it may be experienced in action. The
complexion of our thoughts will be practical, not theoretical.

In a dramatic story in the Book of Numbers faith is seen in action.
Israel became discouraged and spoke against God, and the Lord sent
fiery serpents among them. "And they bit the people; and much people
of Israel died." Then Moses sought the Lord for them and He heard and
gave them a remedy against the bite of the serpents. He commanded
Moses to make a serpent of brass and put it upon a pole in sight of all
the people, "and it shall come to pass, that everyone that is bitten, when
he looketh upon it, shall live." Moses obeyed, "and it came to pass, that
if a serpent had bitten any man, when he beheld the serpent of brass, he
lived" (Num. 21:4-9).

In the New Testament this important bit of history is interpreted
for us by no less an authority than our Lord Jesus Christ Himself. He
is explaining to His hearers how they may be saved. He tells them that
it is by believing. Then to make it clear He refers to this incident in the
Book of Numbers. "As Moses lifted up the serpent in the wilderness,
even so must the Son of man be lifted up: that whosoever believeth in
him should not perish, but have eternal life" (John 3:14-15).

Our plain man in reading this would make an important discovery.
He would notice that "look" and "believe" were synonymous terms.
"Looking" on the Old Testament serpent is identical with "believing"
on the New Testament Christ. That is, the *looking* and the *believing* are
the same thing. And he would understand that while Israel looked with
their external eyes, believing is done with the heart. I think he would
conclude that *faith is the gaze of a soul upon a saving God.*

When he had seen this he would remember passages he had read
before, and their meaning would come flooding over him. "They looked
unto him, and were lightened: and their faces were not ashamed" (Psa.
34:5). "Unto thee lift I up mine eyes, O thou that dwellest in the heavens. Behold, as the eyes of servants look unto the hand of their masters,
and as the eyes of a maiden unto the hand of her mistress; so our eyes
wait upon the Lord our God, until that he have mercy upon us" (Psa.
123:1-2). Here the man seeking mercy looks straight at the God of mercy and never takes his eyes away from Him till mercy is granted. And
our Lord Himself looked always at God. "Looking up to heaven, he

blessed, and brake, and gave the bread to his disciples" (Matt. 14:19). Indeed Jesus taught that He wrought His works by always keeping His inward eyes upon His Father. His power lay in His continuous look at God (John 5:19-21).

In full accord with the few texts we have quoted is the whole tenor of the inspired Word. It is summed up for us in the Hebrew epistle when we are instructed to run life's race "looking unto Jesus the author and finisher of our faith." From all this we learn that faith is not a once-done act, but a continuous gaze of the heart at the Triune God.

Believing, then, is directing the heart's attention to Jesus. It is lifting the mind to "behold the Lamb of God," and never ceasing that beholding for the rest of our lives. At first this may be difficult, but it becomes easier as we look steadily at His wondrous Person, quietly and without strain. Distractions may hinder, but once the heart is committed to Him, after each brief excursion away from Him the attention will return again and rest upon Him like a wandering bird coming back to its window.

I would emphasize this one committal, this one great volitional act which establishes the heart's intention to gaze forever upon Jesus. God takes this intention for our choice and makes what allowances He must for the thousand distractions which beset us in this evil world. He knows that we have set the direction of our hearts toward Jesus, and we can know it too, and comfort ourselves with the knowledge that a habit of soul is forming which will become after a while a sort of spiritual reflex requiring no more conscious effort on our part.

Faith is the least self-regarding of the virtues. It is by its very nature scarcely conscious of its own existence. Like the eye which sees everything in front of it and never sees itself, faith is occupied with the Object upon which it rests and pays no attention to itself at all. While we are looking at God we do not see ourselves—blessed riddance. The man who has struggled to purify himself and has had nothing but repeated failures will experience real relief when he stops tinkering with his soul and looks away to the perfect One. While he looks at Christ the very things he has so long been trying to do will be getting done within him. It will be God working in him to will and to do.

Faith is not in itself a meritorious act; the merit is in the One toward Whom it is directed. Faith is a redirecting of our sight, a getting out of the focus of our own vision and getting God into focus. Sin has twisted our vision inward and made it self-regarding. Unbelief has put self where God should be, and is perilously close to the sin of Lucifer who said, "I will set my throne above the throne of God." Faith looks *out* instead of *in* and the whole life falls into line.

All this may seem too simple. But we have no apology to make. To those who would seek to climb into heaven after help or descend into hell God says, "The word is nigh thee, even the word of faith." The word induces us to lift up our eyes unto the Lord and the blessed work of faith begins.

When we lift our inward eyes to gaze upon God we are sure to meet friendly eyes gazing back at us, for it is written that the eyes of the Lord run to and fro throughout all the earth. The sweet language of experience is "Thou God seest me." When the eyes of the soul looking out meet the eyes of God looking in, heaven has begun right here on this earth.

"When all my endeavour is turned toward Thee because all Thy endeavour is turned toward me; when I look unto Thee alone with all my attention, nor ever turn aside the eyes of my mind, because Thou dost enfold me with Thy constant regard; when I direct my love toward Thee alone because Thou, who art Love's self hast turned Thee toward me alone. And what, Lord, is my life, save that embrace wherein Thy delightsome sweetness doth so lovingly enfold me?"[1] So wrote Nicholas of Cusa four hundred years ago.

I should like to say more about this old man of God. He is not much known today anywhere among Christian believers, and among current Fundamentalists he is known not at all. I feel that we could gain much from a little acquaintance with men of his spiritual flavor and the school of Christian thought which they represent. Christian literature, to be accepted and approved by the evangelical leaders of our times, must follow very closely the same train of thought, a kind of "party line" from which it is scarcely safe to depart. A half-century of this in America has made us smug and content. We imitate each other with slavish devotion and our most strenuous efforts are put forth to try to say the same thing that everyone around us is saying—and yet to find an excuse for saying it, some little safe variation on the approved theme or, if no more, at least a new illustration.

Nicholas was a true follower of Christ, a lover of the Lord, radiant and shining in his devotion to the Person of Jesus. His theology was or-

1 Nicholas of Cusa, *The Vision of God*, E. P. Dutton & Co., Inc., New York, 1928. This and the following quotations used by kind permission of the publishers.

thodox, but fragrant and sweet as everything about Jesus might properly
be expected to be. His conception of eternal life, for instance, is beautiful in itself and, if I mistake not, is nearer in spirit to John 17:3 than that
which is current among us today. Life eternal, says Nicholas, is "nought
other than that blessed regard wherewith Thou never ceasest to behold
me, yea, even the secret places of my soul. With Thee, to behold is to
give life; 'tis unceasingly to impart sweetest love of Thee; 'tis to inflame
me to love of Thee by love's imparting, and to feed me by inflaming,
and by feeding to kindle my yearning, and by kindling to make me drink
of the dew of gladness, and by drinking to infuse in me a fountain of life,
and by infusing to make it increase and endure."[2]

Now, if faith is the gaze of the heart at God, and if this gaze is but
the raising of the inward eyes to meet the all-seeing eyes of God, then
it follows that it is one of the easiest things possible to do. It would be
like God to make the most vital thing easy and place it within the range
of possibility for the weakest and poorest of us.

Several conclusions may fairly be drawn from all this. The simplicity of it, for instance. Since believing is looking, it can be done without
special equipment or religious paraphernalia. God has seen to it that
the one life-and-death essential can never be subject to the caprice of
accident. Equipment can break down or get lost, water can leak away,
records can be destroyed by fire, the minister can be delayed or the
church burn down. All these are external to the soul and are subject to
accident or mechanical failure: but *looking* is of the heart and can be
done successfully by any man standing up or kneeling down or lying in
his last agony a thousand miles from any church.

Since believing is looking it can be done *any time*. No season is
superior to another season for this sweetest of all acts. God never made
salvation depend upon new moons nor holy days or sabbaths. A man is
not nearer to Christ on Easter Sunday than he is, say, on Saturday, Au-
gust 3, or Monday, October 4. As long as Christ sits on the mediatorial
throne every day is a good day and all days are days of salvation.

Neither does *place* matter in this blessed work of believing God. Lift
your heart and let it rest upon Jesus and you are instantly in a sanctuary
though it be a Pullman berth or a factory or a kitchen. You can see God
from anywhere if your mind is set to love and obey Him.

Now, someone may ask, "Is not this of which you speak for special

2 *The Vision of God*

persons such as monks or ministers who have by the nature of their calling more time to devote to quiet meditation? I am a busy worker and have little time to spend alone." I am happy to say that the life I describe is for everyone of God's children regardless of calling. It is, in fact, happily practiced every day by many hard working persons and is beyond the reach of none.

Many have found the secret of which I speak and, without giving much thought to what is going on within them, constantly practice this habit of inwardly gazing upon God. They know that something inside their hearts sees God. Even when they are compelled to withdraw their conscious attention in order to engage in earthly affairs there is within them a secret communion always going on. Let their attention but be released for a moment from necessary business and it flies at once to God again. This has been the testimony of many Christians, so many that even as I state it thus I have a feeling that I am quoting, though from whom or from how many I cannot possibly know.

I do not want to leave the impression that the ordinary means of grace have no value. They most assuredly have. Private prayer should be practiced by every Christian. Long periods of Bible meditation will purify our gaze and direct it; church attendance will enlarge our outlook and increase our love for others. Service and work and activity; all are good and should be engaged in by every Christian. But at the bottom of all these things, giving meaning to them, will be the inward habit of beholding God. A new set of eyes (so to speak) will develop within us enabling us to be looking at God while our outward eyes are seeing the scenes of this passing world.

Someone may fear that we are magnifying private religion out of all proportion, that the "us" of the New Testament is being displaced by a selfish "I." Has it ever occurred to you that one hundred pianos all tuned to the same fork are automatically tuned to each other? They are of one accord by being tuned, not to each other, but to another standard to which each one must individually bow. So one hundred worshippers met together, each one looking away to Christ, are in heart nearer to each other than they could possibly be were they to become "unity" conscious and turn their eyes away from God to strive for closer fellowship. Social religion is perfected when private religion is purified. The body becomes stronger as its members become healthier. The whole Church of God gains when the members that compose it begin to seek a better and a higher life.

All the foregoing presupposes true repentance and a full committal of the life to God. It is hardly necessary to mention this, for only persons who have made such a committal will have read this far.

When the habit of inwardly gazing Godward becomes fixed within us we shall be ushered onto a new level of spiritual life more in keeping with the promises of God and the mood of the New Testament. The Triune God will be our dwelling place even while our feet walk the low road of simple duty here among men. We will have found life's *summum bonum* indeed. "There is the source of all delights that can be desired; not only can nought better be thought out by men and angels, but nought better can exist in mode of being! For it is the absolute maximum of every rational desire, than which a greater cannot be."[3]

* * *

O Lord, I have heard a good word inviting me to look away to Thee and be satisfied. My heart longs to respond, but sin has clouded my vision till I see Thee but dimly. Be pleased to cleanse me in Thine own precious blood, and make me inwardly pure, so that I may with unveiled eyes gaze upon Thee all the days of my earthly pilgrimage. Then shall I be prepared to behold Thee in full splendor in the day when Thou shalt appear to be glorified in Thy saints and admired in all them that believe.

Amen.

---

3 *The Vision of God*

8
RESTORING THE CREATOR-CREATURE RELATION

Be thou exalted, O God, above the heavens; let thy
glory be above all the earth.—Psa. 57:5

It is a truism to say that order in nature depends upon right relationships; to achieve harmony each thing must be in its proper position relative to each other thing. In human life it is not otherwise.

I have hinted before in these chapters that the cause of all our human miseries is a radical moral dislocation, an upset in our relation to God and to each other. For whatever else the Fall may have been, it was most certainly a sharp change in man's relation to his Creator. He adopted toward God an altered attitude, and by so doing destroyed the proper Creator-creature relation in which, unknown to him, his true happiness lay. Essentially salvation is the restoration of a right relation between man and his Creator, a bringing back to normal of the Creator-creature relation.

A satisfactory spiritual life will begin with a complete change in relation between God and the sinner; not a judicial change merely, but a conscious and experienced change affecting the sinner's whole nature. The atonement in Jesus' blood makes such a change judicially possible and the working of the Holy Spirit makes it emotionally satisfying. The story of the prodigal son perfectly illustrates this latter phase. He had brought a world of trouble upon himself by forsaking the position which he had properly held as son of his father. At bottom his restoration was nothing more than a re-establishing of the father-son relation which had existed from his birth and had been altered temporarily by his act of sinful rebellion. This story overlooks the legal aspects of redemption, but it makes beautifully clear the experiential aspects of salvation.

In determining relationships we must begin somewhere. There must be somewhere a fixed center against which everything else is measured, where the law of relativity does not enter and we can say "IS" and make no allowances. Such a center is God. When God would make His Name known to mankind He could find no better word than "I AM." When He speaks in the first person He says, "I AM"; when we speak of Him we say, "He is"; when we speak to Him we say, "Thou art." Everyone and everything else measures from that fixed point. "I am that I am," says God, "I change not."

As the sailor locates his position on the sea by "shooting" the sun, so we may get our moral bearings by looking at God. We must begin with God. We are right when and only when we stand in a right position relative to God, and we are wrong so far and so long as we stand in any other position.

Much of our difficulty as seeking Christians stems from our unwillingness to take God as He is and adjust our lives accordingly. We insist upon trying to modify Him and to bring Him nearer to our own image. The flesh whimpers against the rigor of God's inexorable sentence and begs like Agag for a little mercy, a little indulgence of its carnal ways. It is no use. We can get a right start only by accepting God as He is and learning to love Him for what He is. As we go on to know Him better we shall find it a source of unspeakable joy that God is just what He is. Some of the most rapturous moments we know will be those we spend in reverent admiration of the Godhead. In those holy moments the very thought of change in Him will be too painful to endure.

So let us begin with God. Back of all, above all, before all is God; first in sequential order, above in rank and station, exalted in dignity and honor. As the self-existent One He gave being to all things, and all things exist out of Him and for Him. "Thou art worthy, O Lord, to receive glory and honour and power: for thou hast created all things, and for thy pleasure they are and were created."

Every soul belongs to God and exists by His pleasure. God being Who and What He is, and we being who and what we are, the only thinkable relation between us is one of full lordship on His part and complete submission on ours. We owe Him every honor that it is in our power to give Him. Our everlasting grief lies in giving Him anything less.

The pursuit of God will embrace the labor of bringing our total personality into conformity to His. And this not judicially, but actually. I do not here refer to the act of justification by faith in Christ. I speak of a voluntary exalting of God to His proper station over us and a willing surrender of our whole being to the place of worshipful submission which the Creator-creature circumstance makes proper.

The moment we make up our minds that we are going on with this determination to exalt God over all we step out of the world's parade. We shall find ourselves out of adjustment to the ways of the world, and increasingly so as we make progress in the holy way. We shall acquire a new viewpoint; a new and different psychology will be formed within us; a new power will begin to surprise us by its upsurgings and its outgoings.

Our break with the world will be the direct outcome of our changed relation to God. For the world of fallen men does not honor God. Millions call themselves by His Name, it is true, and pay some token respect to Him, but a simple test will show how little He is really honored among them. Let the average man be put to the proof on the question of who is *above*, and his true position will be exposed. Let him be forced into making a choice between God and money, between God and men, between God and personal ambition, God and self, God and human love, and God will take second place every time. Those other things will be exalted above. However the man may protest, the proof is in the choices he makes day after day throughout his life.

"Be thou exalted" is the language of victorious spiritual experience. It is a little key to unlock the door to great treasures of grace. It is central in the life of God in the soul. Let the seeking man reach a place where life and lips join to say continually "Be thou exalted," and a thousand minor problems will be solved at once. His Christian life ceases to be the complicated thing it had been before and becomes the very essence of simplicity. By the exercise of his will he has set his course, and on that course he will stay as if guided by an automatic pilot. If blown off course for a moment by some adverse wind he will surely return again as by a secret bent of the soul. The hidden motions of the Spirit are working in his favor, and "the stars in their courses" fight for him. He has met his life problem at its center, and everything else must follow along.

Let no one imagine that he will lose anything of human dignity by this voluntary sell-out of his all to his God. He does not by this degrade himself as a man; rather he finds his right place of high honor as one made in the image of his Creator. His deep disgrace lay in his moral derangement, his unnatural usurpation of the place of God. His honor will be proved by restoring again that stolen throne. In exalting God over all he finds his own highest honor upheld.

Anyone who might feel reluctant to surrender his will to the will of another should remember Jesus' words, "Whosoever committeth sin is the servant of sin." We must of necessity be servant to someone, either to God or to sin. The sinner prides himself on his independence, completely overlooking the fact that he is the weak slave of the sins that rule his members. The man who surrenders to Christ exchanges a cruel slave driver for a kind and gentle Master whose yoke is easy and whose burden is light.

Made as we were in the image of God we scarcely find it strange to take again our God as our All. God was our original habitat and our hearts cannot but feel at home when they enter again that ancient and beautiful abode.

I hope it is clear that there is a logic behind God's claim to pre-eminence. That place is His by every right in earth or heaven. While we take to ourselves the place that is His the whole course of our lives is out of joint. Nothing will or can restore order till our hearts make the great decision: God shall be exalted above.

"Them that honour me I will honour," said God once to a priest of Israel, and that ancient law of the Kingdom stands today unchanged by the passing of time or the changes of dispensation. The whole Bible and every page of history proclaim the perpetuation of that law. "If any man serve me, him will my Father honour," said our Lord Jesus, tying in the old with the new and revealing the essential unity of His ways with men.

Sometimes the best way to see a thing is to look at its opposite. Eli and his sons are placed in the priesthood with the stipulation that they honor God in their lives and ministrations. This they fail to do, and God sends Samuel to announce the consequences. Unknown to Eli this law of reciprocal honor has been all the while secretly working, and now the time has come for judgment to fall. Hophni and Phineas, the degenerate priests, fall in battle, the wife of Hophni dies in childbirth, Israel flees before her enemies, the ark of God is captured by the Philistines and the old man Eli falls backward and dies of a broken neck. Thus stark utter tragedy followed upon Eli's failure to honor God.

Now set over against this almost any Bible character who honestly tried to glorify God in his earthly walk. See how God winked at weaknesses and overlooked failures as He poured upon His servants grace and blessing untold. Let it be Abraham, Jacob, David, Daniel, Elijah or whom you will; honor followed honor as harvest the seed. The man of God set his heart to exalt God above all; God accepted his intention as fact and acted accordingly. Not perfection, but holy intention made the difference.

In our Lord Jesus Christ this law was seen in simple perfection. In His lowly manhood He humbled Himself and gladly gave all glory to His Father in heaven. He sought not His own honor, but the honor of God who sent Him. "If I honour myself," He said on one occasion, "my honour is nothing; it is my Father that honoureth me." So far had the proud Pharisees departed from this law that they could not understand one who honored God at his own expense. "I honour my Father," said Jesus to them, "and ye do dishonour me."

Another saying of Jesus, and a most disturbing one, was put in the form of a question, "How can ye believe, which receive honour one of another, and seek not the honour that cometh from God alone?" If I understand this correctly Christ taught here the alarming doctrine that the desire for honor among men made belief impossible. Is this sin at the root of religious unbelief? Could it be that those "intellectual difficulties" which men blame for their inability to believe are but smoke screens to conceal the real cause that lies behind them? Was it this greedy desire for honor from man that made men into Pharisees and Pharisees into Deicides? Is this the secret back of religious self-righteousness and empty worship? I believe it may be. The whole course of the life is upset by failure to put God where He belongs. We exalt ourselves instead of God and the curse follows.

In our desire after God let us keep always in mind that God also hath desire, and His desire is toward the sons of men, and more particularly toward those sons of men who will make the once-for-all decision to exalt Him over all. Such as these are precious to God above all treasures of earth or sea. In them God finds a theater where He can display His exceeding kindness toward us in Christ Jesus. With them God can walk unhindered, toward them He can act like the God He is.

In speaking thus I have one fear; it is that I may convince the mind before God can win the heart. For this God-above-all position is one not easy to take. The mind may approve it while not having the consent of the will to put it into effect. While the imagination races ahead to honor God, the will may lag behind and the man never guess how divided his heart is. The whole man must make the decision before the heart can know any real satisfaction. God wants us all, and He will not rest till He gets us all. No part of the man will do.

Let us pray over this in detail, throwing ourselves at God's feet and meaning everything we say. No one who prays thus in sincerity need wait long for tokens of divine acceptance. God will unveil His glory before His servant's eyes, and He will place all His treasures at the disposal of such a one, for He knows that His honor is safe in such consecrated hands.

*   *   *

O God, be Thou exalted over my possessions. Nothing of earth's treasures shall seem dear unto me if only Thou art glorified in my life. Be Thou exalted over my friendships. I am determined that Thou shalt be above all, though I must stand deserted and alone in the midst of the earth. Be Thou exalted above my comforts. Though it mean the loss of bodily comforts and the carrying of heavy crosses I shall keep my vow made this day before Thee. Be Thou exalted over my reputation. Make me ambitious to please Thee even if as a result I must sink into obscurity and my name be forgotten as a dream. Rise, O Lord, into Thy proper place of honor, above my ambitions, above my likes and dislikes, above my family, my health and even my life itself. Let me decrease that Thou mayest increase, let me sink that Thou mayest rise above. Ride forth upon me as Thou didst ride into Jerusalem mounted upon the humble little beast, a colt, the foal of an ass, and let me hear the children cry to Thee, "Hosanna in the highest."

9
MEEKNESS AND REST

***Blessed are the meek: for they shall inherit the
earth.***—Matt. 5:5

A fairly accurate description of the human race might be furnished
one unacquainted with it by taking the Beatitudes, turning them wrong
side out and saying, "Here is your human race." For the exact opposite
of the virtues in the Beatitudes are the very qualities which distinguish
human life and conduct.

In the world of men we find nothing approaching the virtues of
which Jesus spoke in the opening words of the famous Sermon on the
Mount. Instead of poverty of spirit we find the rankest kind of pride;
instead of mourners we find pleasure seekers; instead of meekness, arrogance; instead of hunger after righteousness we hear men saying, "I
am rich and increased with goods and have need of nothing"; instead of
mercy we find cruelty; instead of purity of heart, corrupt imaginings; instead of peacemakers we find men quarrelsome and resentful; instead of
rejoicing in mistreatment we find them fighting back with every weapon
at their command.

Of this kind of moral stuff civilized society is composed. The atmo-
sphere is charged with it; we breathe it with every breath and drink it
with our mother's milk. Culture and education refine these things slightly but leave them basically untouched. A whole world of literature has
been created to justify this kind of life as the only normal one. And
this is the more to be wondered at seeing that these are the evils which
make life the bitter struggle it is for all of us. All our heartaches and a
great many of our physical ills spring directly out of our sins. Pride,

arrogance, resentfulness, evil imaginings, malice, greed: these are the sources of more human pain than all the diseases that ever afflicted mortal flesh.

Into a world like this the sound of Jesus' words comes wonderful and strange, a visitation from above. It is well that He spoke, for no one else could have done it as well; and it is good that we listen. His words are the essence of truth. He is not offering an opinion; Jesus never uttered opinions. He never guessed; He knew, and He knows. His words are not as Solomon's were, the sum of sound wisdom or the results of keen observation. He spoke out of the fulness of His Godhead, and His words are very Truth itself. He is the only one who could say "blessed" with complete authority, for He is the Blessed One come from the world above to confer blessedness upon mankind. And His words were supported by deeds mightier than any performed on this earth by any other man. It is wisdom for us to listen.

As was often so with Jesus, He used this word "meek" in a brief crisp sentence, and not till some time later did He go on to explain it. In the same book of Matthew He tells us more about it and applies it to our lives. "Come unto me, all ye that labour and are heavy laden, and I will give you rest. Take my yoke upon you, and learn of me; for I am meek and lowly in heart: and ye shall find rest unto your souls. For my yoke is easy, and my burden is light." Here we have two things standing in contrast to each other, a burden and a rest. The burden is not a local one, peculiar to those first hearers, but one which is borne by the whole human race. It consists not of political oppression or poverty or hard work. It is far deeper than that. It is felt by the rich as well as the poor for it is something from which wealth and idleness can never deliver us.

The burden borne by mankind is a heavy and a crushing thing. The word Jesus used means a load carried or toil borne to the point of exhaustion. Rest is simply release from that burden. It is not something we do, it is what comes to us when we cease to do. His own meekness, that is the rest.

Let us examine our burden. It is altogether an interior one. It attacks the heart and the mind and reaches the body only from within. First, there is the burden of *pride*. The labor of self-love is a heavy one indeed. Think for yourself whether much of your sorrow has not arisen from someone speaking slightingly of you. As long as you set yourself up as a little god to which you must be loyal there will be those who will delight to offer affront to your idol. How then can you hope to have inward peace? The heart's fierce effort to protect itself from every slight, to shield its touchy honor from the bad opinion of friend and enemy, will never let the mind have rest. Continue this fight through the years and the burden will become intolerable. Yet the sons of earth are carrying this burden continually, challenging every word spoken against them, cringing under every criticism, smarting under each fancied slight, tossing sleepless if another is preferred before them.

Such a burden as this is not necessary to bear. Jesus calls us to His rest, and meekness is His method. The meek man cares not at all who is greater than he, for he has long ago decided that the esteem of the world is not worth the effort. He develops toward himself a kindly sense of humor and learns to say, "Oh, so you have been overlooked? They have placed someone else before you? They have whispered that you are pretty small stuff after all? And now you feel hurt because the world is saying about you the very things you have been saying about yourself? Only yesterday you were telling God that you were nothing, a mere worm of the dust. Where is your consistency? Come on, humble yourself, and cease to care what men think."

The meek man is not a human mouse afflicted with a sense of his own inferiority. Rather he may be in his moral life as bold as a lion and as strong as Samson; but he has stopped being fooled about himself. He has accepted God's estimate of his own life. He knows he is as weak and helpless as God has declared him to be, but paradoxically, he knows at the same time that he is in the sight of God of more importance than angels. In himself, nothing; in God, everything. That is his motto. He knows well that the world will never see him as God sees him and he has stopped caring. He rests perfectly content to allow God to place His own values. He will be patient to wait for the day when everything will get its own price tag and real worth will come into its own. Then the righteous shall shine forth in the Kingdom of their Father. He is willing to wait for that day.

In the meantime he will have attained a place of soul rest. As he walks on in meekness he will be happy to let God defend him. The old struggle to defend himself is over. He has found the peace which meekness brings.

Then also he will get deliverance from the burden of *pretense*. By this I mean not hypocrisy, but the common human desire to put the best foot forward and hide from the world our real inward poverty. For sin has played many evil tricks upon us, and one has been the infusing into us a false sense of shame. There is hardly a man or woman who dares to be just what he or she is without doctoring up the impression. The fear of being found out gnaws like rodents within their hearts. The man of culture is haunted by the fear that he will some day come upon a man more cultured than himself. The learned man fears to meet a man more learned than he. The rich man sweats under the fear that his clothes or his car or his house will sometime be made to look cheap by comparison with those of another rich man. So-called "society" runs by a motivation not higher than this, and the poorer classes on their level are little better.

Let no one smile this off. These burdens are real, and little by little they kill the victims of this evil and unnatural way of life. And the psychology created by years of this kind of thing makes true meekness seem as unreal as a dream, as aloof as a star. To all the victims of the gnawing disease Jesus says, "Ye must become as little children." For little children do not compare; they receive direct enjoyment from what they have without relating it to something else or someone else. Only as they get older and sin begins to stir within their hearts do jealousy and envy appear. Then they are unable to enjoy what they have if someone else has something larger or better. At that early age does the galling burden come down upon their tender souls, and it never leaves them till Jesus sets them free.

Another source of burden is *artificiality*. I am sure that most people live in secret fear that some day they will be careless and by chance an enemy or friend will be allowed to peep into their poor empty souls. So they are never relaxed. Bright people are tense and alert in fear that they may be trapped into saying something common or stupid. Traveled people are afraid that they may meet some Marco Polo who is able to describe some remote place where they have never been.

This unnatural condition is part of our sad heritage of sin, but in our day it is aggravated by our whole way of life. Advertising is largely based upon this habit of pretense. "Courses" are offered in this or that field of human learning frankly appealing to the victim's desire to shine at a party. Books are sold, clothes and cosmetics are peddled, by playing continually upon this desire to appear what we are not. Artificiality is one curse that will drop away the moment we kneel at Jesus' feet and surrender ourselves to His meekness. Then we will not care what people think of us so long as God is pleased. Then *what we are* will be everything; what we appear will take its place far down the scale of interest for us. Apart from sin we have nothing of which to be ashamed. Only an evil desire to shine makes us want to appear other than we are.

The heart of the world is breaking under this load of pride and pretense. There is no release from our burden apart from the meekness of Christ. Good keen reasoning may help slightly, but so strong is this vice that if we push it down one place it will come up somewhere else. To men and women everywhere Jesus says, "Come unto me, and I will give you rest." The rest He offers is the rest of meekness, the blessed relief which comes when we accept ourselves for what we are and cease to pretend. It will take some courage at first, but the needed grace will come as we learn that we are sharing this new and easy yoke with the strong Son of God Himself. He calls it "my yoke," and He walks at one end while we walk at the other.

*   *   *

Lord, make me childlike. Deliver me from the urge to compete with another for place or prestige or position. I would be simple and artless as a little child. Deliver me from pose and pretense. Forgive me for thinking of myself. Help me to forget myself and find my true peace in beholding Thee. That Thou mayest answer this prayer I humble myself before Thee. Lay upon me Thy easy yoke of self-forgetfulness that through it I may find rest.

Amen.

10
THE SACRAMENT OF LIVING

***Whether therefore ye eat, or drink, or whatsoever ye
do, do all to the glory of God.***—I Cor. 10:31

One of the greatest hindrances to internal peace which the Christian
encounters is the common habit of dividing our lives into two areas, the
sacred and the secular. As these areas are conceived to exist apart from
each other and to be morally and spiritually incompatible, and as we are
compelled by the necessities of living to be always crossing back and
forth from the one to the other, our inner lives tend to break up so that
we live a divided instead of a unified life.

Our trouble springs from the fact that we who follow Christ inhabit
at once two worlds, the spiritual and the natural. As children of Adam
we live our lives on earth subject to the limitations of the flesh and the
weaknesses and ills to which human nature is heir. Merely to live among
men requires of us years of hard toil and much care and attention to the
things of this world. In sharp contrast to this is our life in the Spirit.
There we enjoy another and higher kind of life; we are children of God;
we possess heavenly status and enjoy intimate fellowship with Christ.

This tends to divide our total life into two departments. We come
unconsciously to recognize two sets of actions. The first are performed
with a feeling of satisfaction and a firm assurance that they are pleasing
to God. These are the sacred acts and they are usually thought to be
prayer, Bible reading, hymn singing, church attendance and such other
acts as spring directly from faith. They may be known by the fact that
they have no direct relation to this world, and would have no meaning
whatever except as faith shows us another world, "an house not made
with hands, eternal in the heavens."

Over against these sacred acts are the secular ones. They include all of the ordinary activities of life which we share with the sons and daughters of Adam: eating, sleeping, working, looking after the needs of the body and performing our dull and prosaic duties here on earth. These we often do reluctantly and with many misgivings, often apologizing to God for what we consider a waste of time and strength. The upshot of this is that we are uneasy most of the time. We go about our common tasks with a feeling of deep frustration, telling ourselves pensively that there's a better day coming when we shall slough off this earthly shell and be bothered no more with the affairs of this world.

This is the old sacred-secular antithesis. Most Christians are caught in its trap. They cannot get a satisfactory adjustment between the claims of the two worlds. They try to walk the tight rope between two kingdoms and they find no peace in either. Their strength is reduced, their outlook confused and their joy taken from them.

I believe this state of affairs to be wholly unnecessary. We have gotten ourselves on the horns of a dilemma, true enough, but the dilemma is not real. It is a creature of misunderstanding. The sacred-secular antithesis has no foundation in the New Testament. Without doubt a more perfect understanding of Christian truth will deliver us from it.

The Lord Jesus Christ Himself is our perfect example, and He knew no divided life. In the Presence of His Father He lived on earth without strain from babyhood to His death on the cross. God accepted the offering of His total life, and made no distinction between act and act. "I do always the things that please him," was His brief summary of His own life as it related to the Father. As He moved among men He was poised and restful. What pressure and suffering He endured grew out of His position as the world's sin bearer; they were never the result of moral uncertainty or spiritual maladjustment.

Paul's exhortation to "do all to the glory of God" is more than pious idealism. It is an integral part of the sacred revelation and is to be accepted as the very Word of Truth. It opens before us the possibility of making every act of our lives contribute to the glory of God. Lest we should be too timid to include everything, Paul mentions specifically eating and drinking. This humble privilege we share with the beasts that perish. If these lowly animal acts can be so performed as to honor God, then it becomes difficult to conceive of one that cannot.

That monkish hatred of the body which figures so prominently in the works of certain early devotional writers is wholly without support in the Word of God. Common modesty is found in the Sacred Scriptures, it is true, but never prudery or a false sense of shame. The New Testament accepts as a matter of course that in His incarnation our Lord took upon Him a real human body, and no effort is made to steer around the downright implications of such a fact. He lived in that body here among men and never once performed a non-sacred act. His presence in human flesh sweeps away forever the evil notion that there is about the human body something innately offensive to the Deity. God created our bodies, and we do not offend Him by placing the responsibility where it belongs. He is not ashamed of the work of His own hands.

Perversion, misuse and abuse of our human powers should give us cause enough to be ashamed. Bodily acts done in sin and contrary to nature can never honor God. Wherever the human will introduces moral evil we have no longer our innocent and harmless powers as God made them; we have instead an abused and twisted thing which can never bring glory to its Creator.

Let us, however, assume that perversion and abuse are not present. Let us think of a Christian believer in whose life the twin wonders of repentance and the new birth have been wrought. He is now living according to the will of God as he understands it from the written Word. Of such a one it may be said that every act of his life is or can be as truly sacred as prayer or baptism or the Lord's Supper. To say this is not to bring all acts down to one dead level; it is rather to lift every act up into a living kingdom and turn the whole life into a sacrament.

If a sacrament is an external expression of an inward grace than we need not hesitate to accept the above thesis. By one act of consecration of our total selves to God we can make every subsequent act express that consecration. We need no more be ashamed of our body—the fleshly servant that carries us through life—than Jesus was of the humble beast upon which He rode into Jerusalem. "The Lord hath need of him" may well apply to our mortal bodies. If Christ dwells in us we may bear about the Lord of glory as the little beast did of old and give occasion to the multitudes to cry, "Hosanna in the highest."

That we *see* this truth is not enough. If we would escape from the toils of the sacred-secular dilemma the truth must "run in our blood" and condition the complexion of our thoughts. We must practice living to the glory of God, actually and determinedly. By meditation upon this truth, by talking it over with God often in our prayers, by recalling it to our minds frequently as we move about among men, a *sense* of its wondrous meaning will begin to take hold of us. The old painful duality will go down before a restful unity of life. The knowledge that we are all God's, that He has received all and rejected nothing, will unify our inner lives and make everything sacred to us.

This is not quite all. Long-held habits do not die easily. It will take intelligent thought and a great deal of reverent prayer to escape completely from the sacred-secular psychology. For instance it may be difficult for the average Christian to get hold of the idea that his daily labors can be performed as acts of worship acceptable to God by Jesus Christ. The old antithesis will crop up in the back of his head sometimes to disturb his peace of mind. Nor will that old serpent the devil take all this lying down. He will be there in the cab or at the desk or in the field to remind the Christian that he is giving the better part of his day to the things of this world and allotting to his religious duties only a trifling portion of his time. And unless great care is taken this will create confusion and bring discouragement and heaviness of heart.

We can meet this successfully only by the exercise of an aggressive faith. We must offer all our acts to God and believe that He accepts them. Then hold firmly to that position and keep insisting that every act of every hour of the day and night be included in the transaction. Keep reminding God in our times of private prayer that we mean every act for His glory; then supplement those times by a thousand thought-prayers as we go about the job of living. Let us practice the fine art of making every work a priestly ministration. Let us believe that God is in all our simple deeds and learn to find Him there.

A concomitant of the error which we have been discussing is the sacred-secular antithesis as applied to places. It is little short of astonishing that we can read the New Testament and still believe in the inherent sacredness of places as distinguished from other places. This error is so widespread that one feels all alone when he tries to combat it. It has acted as a kind of dye to color the thinking of religious persons and has colored the eyes as well so that it is all but impossible to detect its fallacy. In the face of every New Testament teaching to the contrary it has been said and sung throughout the centuries and accepted as a part of the Christian message, the which it most surely is not. Only the Quakers, so far as my knowledge goes, have had the perception to see the error and the courage to expose it.

Here are the facts as I see them. For four hundred years Israel had dwelt in Egypt, surrounded by the crassest idolatry. By the hand of Moses they were brought out at last and started toward the land of promise. The very idea of holiness had been lost to them. To correct this, God began at the bottom. He localized Himself in the cloud and fire and later when the tabernacle had been built He dwelt in fiery manifestation in the Holy of Holies. By innumerable distinctions God taught Israel the difference between holy and unholy. There were holy days, holy vessels, holy garments. There were washings, sacrifices, offerings of many kinds. By these means Israel learned that *God is holy*. It was this that He was teaching them. Not the holiness of things or places, but the holiness of Jehovah was the lesson they must learn.

Then came the great day when Christ appeared. Immediately He began to say, "Ye have heard that it was said by them of old time—but *I* say unto you." The Old Testament schooling was over. When Christ died on the cross the veil of the temple was rent from top to bottom. The Holy of Holies was opened to everyone who would enter in faith. Christ's words were remembered, "The hour cometh, when ye shall neither in this mountain, nor yet at Jerusalem, worship the Father.... But the hour cometh, and now is, when the true worshippers shall worship the Father in spirit and in truth: for the Father seeketh such to worship Him. God is Spirit, and they that worship him must worship him in spirit and in truth."

Shortly after, Paul took up the cry of liberty and declared all meats clean, every day holy, all places sacred and every act acceptable to God. The sacredness of times and places, a half-light necessary to the education of the race, passed away before the full sun of spiritual worship.

The essential spirituality of worship remained the possession of the Church until it was slowly lost with the passing of the years. Then the natural *legality* of the fallen hearts of men began to introduce the old distinctions. The Church came to observe again days and seasons and times. Certain places were chosen and marked out as holy in a special sense. Differences were observed between one and another day or place or person, "The sacraments" were first two, then three, then four until with the triumph of Romanism they were fixed at seven.

In all charity, and with no desire to reflect unkindly upon any Christian, however misled, I would point out that the Roman Catholic church represents today the sacred-secular heresy carried to its logical conclusion. Its deadliest effect is the complete cleavage it introduces between religion and life. Its teachers attempt to avoid this snare by many footnotes and multitudinous explanations, but the mind's instinct for logic is too strong. In practical living the cleavage is a fact.

From this bondage reformers and puritans and mystics have labored to free us. Today the trend in conservative circles is back toward that bondage again. It is said that a horse after it has been led out of a burning building will sometimes by a strange obstinacy break loose from its rescuer and dash back into the building again to perish in the flame. By some such stubborn tendency toward error Fundamentalism in our day is moving back toward spiritual slavery. The observation of days and times is becoming more and more prominent among us. "Lent" and "holy week" and "good" Friday are words heard more and more frequently upon the lips of gospel Christians. We do not know when we are well off.

In order that I may be understood and not be misunderstood I would throw into relief the practical implications of the teaching for which I have been arguing, i.e., the sacramental quality of every day living. Over against its positive meanings I should like to point out a few things it does not mean.

It does not mean, for instance, that everything we do is of equal importance with everything else we do or may do. One act of a good man's life may differ widely from another in importance. Paul's sewing of tents was not equal to his writing of an Epistle to the Romans, but both were accepted of God and both were true acts of worship. Certainly it is more important to lead a soul to Christ than to plant a garden, but the planting of the garden *can* be as holy an act as the winning of a soul.

Again, it does not mean that every man is as useful as every other man. Gifts differ in the body of Christ. A Billy Bray is not to be compared with a Luther or a Wesley for sheer usefulness to the Church and to the world; but the service of the less gifted brother is as pure as that of the more gifted, and God accepts both with equal pleasure.

The "layman" need never think of his humbler task as being inferior to that of his minister. Let every man abide in the calling wherein he is called and his work will be as sacred as the work of the ministry. It is not what a man does that determines whether his work is sacred or secular, it is *why* he does it. The motive is everything. Let a man sanctify the Lord God in his heart and he can thereafter do no common act. All he does is good and acceptable to God through Jesus Christ. For such a man, living itself will be sacramental and the whole world a sanctuary. His entire life will be a priestly ministration. As he performs his never so simple task he will hear the voice of the seraphim saying, "Holy, Holy, Holy, is the Lord of hosts: the whole earth is full of his glory."

*　*　*

Lord, I would trust Thee completely; I would be altogether Thine; I would exalt Thee above all. I desire that I may feel no sense of possessing anything outside of Thee. I want constantly to be aware of Thy overshadowing Presence and to hear Thy speaking Voice. I long to live in restful sincerity of heart. I want to live so fully in the Spirit that all my thought may be as sweet incense ascending to Thee and every act of my life may be an act of worship. Therefore I pray in the words of Thy great servant of old, "I beseech Thee so for to cleanse the intent of mine heart with the unspeakable gift of Thy grace, that I may perfectly love Thee and worthily praise Thee." And all this I confidently believe Thou wilt grant me through the merits of Jesus Christ Thy Son.

Amen.

MAN

–

THE DWELLING PLACE OF GOD

PREFACE

The supreme interest in the life of A. W. Tozer was God: He who spoke and brought the world into being, Who justly rules over men and nations, yet deigns to make man His dwelling place. He believed that all that really matters is for man to be in right relationship with God, that his first duty-and privilege-is "to glorify God and enjoy Him forever." For this reason he delighted to speak to men of God's majesty and wonder and grace and he ever sought to instruct and exhort Christians to let this be the purpose of their lives. He grieved that they should be content with less.

Nothing he preached or wrote was merely academic or theoretical. What he said about God came out of many hours spent in His presence and with His Word. What he wrote about men was what he knew of his own heart and observed in others. With the Spirit's anointing came discernment; perception and clarity issued out of a disciplined mind. A broad knowledge averted dullness, and a lively wit brought freshness.

The chapters in this book deal with many aspects of one subject: the relationship of God and man. They are above all practical and all who read them will profit.

1
MAN – THE DWELLING PLACE OF GOD

Deep inside every man there is a private sanctum where dwells the mysterious essence of his being. This far-in reality is that in the man which is what it is of itself without reference to any other part of the man's complex nature. It is the man's "I Am," a gift from the I AM who created him.

The I AM which is God is underived and selfexistent; the "I Am" which is man is derived from God and dependent every moment upon His creative fiat for its continued existence. One is the Creator, high over all, ancient of days, dwelling in light unapproachable. The other is a creature and, though privileged beyond all others, is still but a creature, a pensioner on God's bounty and a suppliant before His throne.

The deep-in human entity of which we speak is called in the Scriptures the spirit of man. "For what man knoweth the things of man, save the spirit of man which is in him? even so the things of God knoweth no man, but the Spirit of God" (I Cor. 2:11) . As God's self-knowledge lies in the eternal Spirit, so man's selfknowledge is by his own spirit, and his knowledge of God is by the direct impression of the Spirit of God upon the spirit of man.

The importance of all this cannot be overestimated as we think and study and pray. It reveals the essential spirituality of mankind. It denies that man is a creature having a spirit and declares that he is a spirit having a body. That which makes him a human being is not his body but his spirit, in which the image of God originally lay.

One of the most liberating declarations in the New Testament is this: "The true worshippers shall worship the Father in spirit and in truth:

for the Father seeketh such to worship him. God is a Spirit: and they that worship him must worship him in spirit and in truth" (John 4:23, 24) . Here the nature of worship is shown to be wholly spiritual. True religion is removed from diet and days, from garments and ceremonies, and placed where it belongs-in the union of the spirit of man with the Spirit of God.

From man's standpoint the most tragic loss suffered in the Fall was the vacating of this inner sanctum by the Spirit of God. At the far-in hidden center of man's being is a bush fitted to be the dwelling place of the Triune God. There God planned to rest and glow with moral and spiritual fire. Man by his sin forfeited this indescribably wonderful privilege and must now dwell there alone. For so intimately private is the place that no creature can intrude; no one can enter but Christ; and He will enter only by the invitation of faith. "Behold, I stand at the door, and knock: if any man hear my voice, and open the door, I will come in to him, and will sup with him, and he with me" (Rev. 3:20).

By the mysterious operation of the Spirit in the new birth, that which is called by Peter "the divine nature" enters the deep-in core of the believer's heart and establishes residence there. "If any man have not the Spirit of Christ, he is none of his," for "the Spirit itself beareth witness with our spirit, that we are the children of God" (Rom. 8:9, 16). Such a one is a true Christian, and only such. Baptism, confirmation, the receiving of the sacraments, church membership-these mean nothing unless the supreme act of God in regeneration also takes place. Religious externals may have a meaning for the God-inhabited soul; for any others they are not only useless but may actually become snares, deceiving them into a false and perilous sense of security.

"Keep thy heart with all diligence" is more than a wise saying; it is a solemn charge laid upon us by the One who cares most about us. To it we should give the most careful heed lest at any time we should let it slip.

2
THE CALL OF CHRIST

To be called to follow Christ is a high honor; higher indeed than any honor men can bestow upon each other.

Were all the nations of the earth to unite in one great federation and call a man to head that federation, that man would be honored above any other man that ever lived. Yet the humblest man who heeds the call to follow Christ has an honor far above such a man; for the nations of the earth can bestow only such honor as they possess, while the honor of Christ is supreme over all. God has given Him a name that is above every name.

This being true and being known to the heavenly intelligences, the methods we use to persuade men to follow Christ must seem to them extremely illogical if not downright wrong.

Evangelical Christians commonly offer Christ to mankind as a nostrum to cure their ills, a way out of their troubles, a quick and easy means to the achievement of personal ends. They use the right words, but their emphasis is awry. The message is so presented as to leave the hearer with the impression that he is being asked to give up much to gain more. And that is not good, however well intentioned it may be.

What we do is precisely what a good salesman does when he presents the excellence of his product as compared with that of his closest competitor. The customer chooses the better of the two, as who would not? But the weakness of the whole salesmanship technique is apparent: the idea of selfish gain is present in the whole transaction.

Jesus Christ is a Man come to save men. In Him the divine nature is married to our human nature, and wherever human nature exists there is the raw material out of which He makes followers and saints. Our Lord recognizes no classes, high or low, rich or poor, old or young, man or woman: all are human and all are alike to Him. His invitation is to all mankind.

In New Testament times persons from many and varied social levels heard His call and responded: Peter the fisherman; Levi the publican; Luke the physician; Paul the scholar; Mary the demon possessed; Lydia the businesswoman; Paulus the statesman. A few great and many common persons came. They all came and our Lord received them all in the same way and on the same terms.

From any and every profession or occupation men and women may come if they will. The simple rule is that if the occupation is good, continue in it if you so desire; if it is bad, abandon it at once and seek another. If the call includes detachment from all common pursuits to give full time to the work of the gospel, then no profession or occupation, no matter how good or how noble, must keep us from obeying the call.

The activities in which men engage may be divided into two categories: the morally bad and the morally neutral. The activities of the burglar, the gambler, the dictator, the procurer, the dope addict, the gangster and all who prey upon society are bad; nothing can make them better. The call of Christ is away from all such. This is not to be questioned or debated, but accepted without delay and acted upon at once.

But the majority of our human activities are not evil in themselves; they are neutral. The laborer, the statesman, the housewife, the doctor, the teacher, the engineer-such as these engage in activities that are neither good nor bad. Their moral qualities are imparted by the one who engages in them. So the call of Christ is not away from such things, for they may be sanctified by the prayer and faith of the individual, and thus turned into a positive good.

One thing is certain: the call of Christ is always a promotion. Were Christ to call a king from his throne to preach the gospel to some tribe of aborigines, that king would be elevated above anything he had known before. Any movement toward Christ is ascent, and any direction away from Him is down.

Yet though we recognize the honor bestowed upon us, there is no place for pride, for the follower of Christ must shoulder his cross and a cross is an object of shame and a symbol of rejection.

Before God and the angels it is a great honor to follow Christ, but before men it is not so. The Christ the world pretends now to honor was once rejected and crucified by that same world. The great saint is honored only after he is dead. Rarely is he known as a saint while he lives. The plaudits of the world come too late, when he can no longer hear them; and perhaps it is better that way. Not many are selfless enough to endure honor without injury to their souls.

In those early Galilean days Christ's followers heard His call, forsook the old life, attached themselves to Him, began to obey His teachings and joined themselves to His band of disciples. This total commitment was their confirmation of faith. Nothing less would do.

And it is not different today. He calls us to leave the old life and to begin the new. There must never be any vacuum, never any place of neutrality where the world cannot identify us. Peter warming himself at the world's fire and trying to seem unconcerned is an example of the kind of halfway discipleship too many are satisfied with. The martyr leaping up in the arena, demanding to be thrown to the lions along with his suffering brethren, is an example of the only kind of dedication that God approves.

3
WHAT WE THINK OF OURSELVES IS IMPORTANT

The man who is seriously convinced that he deserves to go to hell is not likely to go there, while the man who believes that he is worthy of heaven will certainly never enter that blessed place.

I use the word "seriously" to accent true conviction and to distinguish it from mere nominal belief.

It is possible to go through life believing that we believe, while actually having no conviction more vital than a conventional creed inherited from our ancestors or picked up from the general religious notions current in our social circle. If this creed requires that we admit our own depravity we do so and feel proud of our fidelity to the Christian faith. But from the way we love, praise and pamper ourselves it is plain enough that we do not consider ourselves worthy of damnation.

A revealing proof of this is seen in the squeamish way religious writers use words. An amusing example is found in a cautious editorial change made in the song "The Comforter Has Come." One stanza reads:

> "O boundless love divine!
> How shall this tongue of mine,
> To wondering mortals tell
> The matchless grace divine -
> That I, a child of hell,
> Should in His image shine!"

That is how Dr. Bottome felt it and that is how he wrote it; and the man who has seen the holiness of God and the pollution of his own heart will sing it as it was written, for his whole inner life will respond to the experience. Even if he cannot find chapter and verse to brand hint a child of hell, Ins heart indicts him and he eagerly accuses himself before God as fit only for perdition. This is to experience something profounder than theology, more painfully intimate than creed, and while bitter and harsh it is true to the man's Spirit illuminated view of himself. In so confessing, the enlightened heart is being faithful to the terrible fact while it is singing its own condemnation. This I believe is greatly pleasing to God.

It is, I repeat, amusing if somewhat distressing to come upon an editorial change in this song, which was made obviously in the interest of correct theology, but is once removed from reality and twice removed from true moral feeling. In one hymnal it is made to read,

> "That I a child of sin
> Should in His image shine!"

The fastidious song cobbler who made that alteration simply could not think of himself as ever having been a "child of hell." A finicky choice of words sometimes tells us more about a man than the man knows about himself.

This one instance, if isolated in Christian literature, ought not be too significant, but when this kind of thing occurs everywhere as thick as dandelions in a meadow it becomes highly significant indeed. The mincing religious prudery heard in the average pulpit is all a part of this same thing-- art unwillingness to admit the depths of our inner depravity. We do not actually assent to God's judgement of us except as we hold it as a superficial creed. When the pressure is on we back out. A child of sin? Maybe. A child of hell? No.

Our Lord -told of two men who appeared before God in prayer, a Pharisee who recited his virtues and a publican who beat on his breast and pleaded for mercy. The first was rejected, the other justified.

We manage to live with that story in some degree of comfort only by keeping it at full arm's length and never permitting it to catch hold of our conscience. These two men are long ago dead and their story has become it little religious classic. We are different, and how can anything so remote apply to us? So we reason on a level only slightly above our unconscious, and draw what comfort we can from the vagueness and remoteness of it all.

But why should we not face up to it? The truth is that this happened not a long while ago, but yesterday, this morning; not far-away, but here where some of us last knelt to pray. These two men are not dead, but alive, and are found in the local church, at the missionary convention and the deeper life conference here, now, today.

Every man lives at last by his secret philosophy as an airplane flies on its electric beam. It is the profound conviction that we are wholly unworthy of future blessedness, that, we are indeed by nature fitted only for destruction, that leads to true repentance. The man who inwardly believes that lie is too good to perish will certainly perish unless he experiences a radical change of heart about himself.

The poor quality of Christian that grows out of our modern evangelistic meeting may be accounted for by the absence of real repentance accompanying the initial spiritual experience of the converts. And the absence of repentance is the result of an inadequate view of sin and sinfulness held by those who present themselves in the inquiry room.

"No fears, no grace," said Bunyan. "Though there is not always grace where there is fear of hell, yet, to be sure, there is no grace where there is no fear of God." And again, "I care not at all for that profession which begins not in heaviness of mind .... For the fear of God is the beginning of wisdom, and they that lack the beginning have neither middle nor end."

4

THE ONCE-BORN AND THE
TWICE-BORN

Classification is one of the most difficult of all tasks. Even in the realm of religion there are enough lights and shades to make it injudicious to draw too fine a line between men and men. If the religious world were composed of squares of solid black and solid white classification would be easy; but unfortunately it is not.

It is a grave error for us evangelicals to assume that the children of God are all in our communion and that all who are not associated with us are ipso facto enemies of the Lord. The Pharisees made that mistake and crucified Christ as a consequence.

With all this in mind, and leaning over backwards to be fair and charitable, there is yet one distinction which we dare make, which indeed we must make if we are to think the thoughts of God after Him and bring our beliefs into harmony with the Holy Scriptures. That distinction is the one which exists between two classes of human beings, the once-born and the twice-born.

That such a distinction does in fact exist was taught by our Lord with great plainness of speech, in contexts which preclude the possibility that He was merely speaking figuratively. "Except a man be born again, he cannot see the kingdom of God," He said, and the whole chapter where these words are found confirms that He was speaking precisely, setting forth meanings as blunt and downright as it is possible for language to convey.

"Ye must be born again," said Christ. "That which is born of the flesh is flesh; and that which is born of the Spirit is spirit." This clear line of demarcation runs through the entire New Testament, quite literally dividing one human being from another and making a distinction as sharp as that which exists between different genera of the animal kingdom.

Just who belongs to one class and who to the other it is not always possible to judge, though the two kinds of life ordinarily separate from each other. Those who are twice-born crystallize around the Person of Christ and cluster together in companies, while the once-born are held together only by the ties of nature, aided by the ties of race or by common political and social interests.

Our Lord warned His disciples that they would be persecuted. "In the world ye shall have tribulation," He said, and "Blessed are they which are persecuted for righteousness' sake: for theirs is the kingdom of heaven. Blessed are ye, when men shall revile you, and persecute you, and shall say all manner of evil against you falsely, for my sake."

These are only two of many passages of the New Testament warning of persecution or recording the fact of harassment and attack suffered by the followers of the Lord. This same idea runs through the entire Bible from the once-born Cain who slew the twice-born Abel to the Book of the Revelation where the end of human history comes in a burst of blood and fire.

That hostility exists between the once-born and the twice-born is known to every student of the Bible; the reason for it was stated by Christ when He said, "If ye were of the world, the world would love his own: but because ye are not of the world, but I have chosen you out of the world, therefore the world hateth you." The rule was laid down by the apostle Paul when he wrote, "But as then he that was born after the flesh persecuted him that was born after the Spirit, even so it is now."

Difference of moral standards between the onceborn and the twice-born, and their opposite ways of life, may be contributing causes of this hostility; but the real cause lies deeper. There are two spirits abroad in the earth: the spirit that works in the children of disobedience and the Spirit of God. These two can never be reconciled in time or in eternity. The spirit that dwells in the once-born is forever opposed to the Spirit that inhabits the heart of the twice-born. This hostility began somewhere in the remote past before the creation of man and continues to this day. The modern effort to bring peace between these two spirits is not only futile but contrary to the moral laws of the universe.

To teach that the spirit of the once-born is at enmity with the Spirit of the twice-born is to bring down upon one's head every kind of violent abuse. No language is too bitter to hurl against the conceited bigot who would dare to draw such a line of distinction between men. Such malignant ideas are at odds with the brotherhood of man, says the once-born, and are held only by the apostles of disunity and hate. This mighty rage against the twice-born only serves to confirm the truth they teach. But this no one seems to notice.

What we need to restore power to the Christian testimony is not soft talk about brotherhood but an honest recognition that two human races occupy the earth simultaneously: a fallen race that sprang from the loins of Adam and a regenerate race that is born of the Spirit through the redemption which is in Christ Jesus.

To accept this truth requires a tough-mindedness and a spiritual maturity that modern Christians simply do not possess. To face up to it hardly contributes to that "peace of mind" after which our religious weaklings bleat so plaintively.

For myself, I long ago decided that I would rather know the truth than be happy in ignorance. If I cannot have both truth and happiness, give me truth. We'll have a long time to be happy in heaven.

5
ON THE ORIGIN AND NATURE OF THINGS

The celebrated prayer of the great German astronomer, Kepler, has been a benediction to many: "O God, I thank Thee that Thou hast permitted me to think Thy thoughts after Thee."

This prayer is theologically sound because it acknowledges the priority of God in the universe. "In the beginning God" is undoubtedly the most important sentence in the Bible. It is in God that all things begin, and all thoughts as well. In the words of Augustine, "But Thou, O Lord, who ever livest, and in whom nothing dies, since before the world was, and, indeed, before all that can be called `before,' Thou existest, and art the God and Lord of all creatures; and with Thee fixedly abide the causes of all unstable things and the changing sources of all things changeable, and the eternal reasons of all things reasoning and temporal."

Whatever new thing anyone discovers is already old, for it is 1-tt the present expression of a previous thought of God. The idea of the thing precedes the thing itself; and when things raise thoughts in the thinker's mind these are the ancient thoughts of God, however imperfectly understood.

When a true thought enters any man's mind, be he saint or sinner, it must of necessity be God's thought, for God is the origin of all true thoughts and things. That is why many real truths are spoken and written by persons other than Christians. Should an atheist, for instance, state that two times two equals four, he would be stating a truth and thinking God's thought after Him, even though he might deny that God exists at all.

In their search for facts men have confused truths with truth. The words of Christ, "Ye shall know the truth, and the truth shall make you free," have been wrenched from their context and used to stir people to the pursuit of knowledge of many kinds with the expectation of being made "free" by knowledge. Certainly this is not what Christ had in mind when He uttered the words.

Such truths as men discover in the earth beneath and in the astronomic heavens above are properly not truths but facts. We call them truths, as I do here, but they are no more than parts of the jigsaw puzzle of the universe, and when correctly fitted together they provide at least a hint of what the vaster picture is like. But I repeat, they are not truth, and more important, they are not the truth. Were every missing piece discovered and laid in place we would still not have the truth, for the truth is not a composite of thoughts and things. The truth should be spelled with a capital T, for it is nothing less than the Son of God, the Second Person of the blessed Godhead.

The human mind requires an answer to the question concerning the origin and nature of things. The world as we find it must be accounted for in some way. Philosophers and scientists have sought to account for it, the one by speculation, the other by observation, and in their labors they have come upon many useful and inspiring facts. But they have not found the final Truth. That comes by revelation and illumination.

They who believe the Christian revelation know that the universe is a creation. It is not eternal, since it had a beginning, and it is not the result of a succession of happy coincidences whereby an all but infinite number of matching parts accidentally found each other, fell into place and began to hum. So to believe would require a degree of credulity few persons possess. "I had rather believe all the fables in the Legend, and the Talmud, and the Alcoram," said Bacon, "than that this universal frame is without a mind. And therefore God never wrought miracles to convince atheism, because His ordinary works convince it."

Those who have faith are not thrown back upon speculation for the secret of the universe. Faith is an organ of knowledge. "Through faith we understand that the worlds were framed by the word of God, so that things which are seen were not made of things which do appear." The voice of Eternal Wisdom declares, "In the beginning God created" and "In the beginning was the Word .... All things were made by him; and without him was not any thing made that was made."

All things came out of the Word, which in the New Testament means the thought and will of God in active expression and is identified with our Lord Jesus Christ. It is the Son who is the Truth that makes men free.

Not facts, not scientific knowledge, but eternal Truth delivers men, and that eternal Truth became flesh to dwell among us. "This is life eternal, that they might know thee the only true God, and Jesus Christ, whom thou hast sent."

Not only the origin of things is revealed, but the nature of things as well. Because the origin of all things is spirit, all things are at bottom spiritual also. This is a moral universe; it is governed by moral laws and will be judged by moral laws at last. Man above all creatures possesses moral perception and is answerable to the spiritual laws that pervade and sustain the world. Pure materialism-that is, the doctrine that matter is the primordial constituent of the universe is not natural to the human mind. It requires a chronic violation of our basic instincts to accept it as an explanation of the nature of things. And Paul tells us in the first two chapters of his Epistle to the Romans how men get into a state of mind to accept such falsehood.

6
WHY PEOPLE FIND THE BIBLE DIFFICULT

That many persons find the Bible hard to understand will not be denied by those acquainted with the facts. Testimony to the difficulties encountered in Bible reading is too full and too widespread to be dismissed lightly.

In human experience there is usually a complex of causes rather than but one cause for everything, and so it is with the difficulty we run into with the Bible. To the question, Why is the Bible hard to understand? no snap answer can be given; the pert answer is sure to be the wrong one. The problem is multiple instead of singular, and for this reason the effort to find a single solution to it will be disappointing.

In spite of this I venture to give a short answer to the question, and while it is not the whole answer it is a major one and probably contains within itself most of the answers to what must be an involved and highly complex question. 1 believe that we find the Bible difficult because we try to read it as we would read any other book, and it is not the same as any other book.

The Bible is not addressed to just anybody. Its message is directed to a chosen few. Whether these few are chosen by God in a sovereign act of election or are chosen because they meet certain qualifying conditions I leave to each one to decide as he may, knowing full well that his decision will be determined by his basic beliefs about such matters as predestination, free will, the eternal decrees and other related doctrines. But whatever may have taken place in eternity, it is obvious what happens in time: Some believe and some do not; some are morally receptive and some are not; some have spiritual capacity and some have not. It is to those who do and are and have that the Bible is addressed. Those who do not and are not and have not will read it in vain.

Right here I expect some readers to enter strenuous objections, and for reasons not hard to find. Chrisianity today is man-centered, not God-centered. God is made to wait patiently, even respectfully, on the whims of men. The image of God currently popular is that of a distracted Father, struggling in heartbroken desperation to get people to accept a Saviour of whom they feel no need and in whom they have very little interest. To persuade these self-sufficient souls to respond to His generous offers God will do almost anything, even using salesmanship methods and talking down to them in the chummiest way imaginable. This view of things is, of course, a kind of religious romanticism which, while it often uses flattering and sometimes embarassing terms in praise of God, manages nevertheless to make man the star of the show.

The notion that the Bible is addressed to everybody has wrought confusion within and without the church. The effort to apply the teaching of the Sermon on the Mount to the unregenerate nations of the world is one example of this. Courts of law and the military powers of the earth are urged to follow the teachings of Christ, an obviously impossible thing for them to do. To quote the words of Christ as guides for policemen, judges and generals is to misunderstand those words completely and to reveal a total lack of understanding of the purposes of divine revelation. The gracious words of Christ are for the sons and daughters of grace, not for the Gentile nations whose chosen symbols are the lion, the eagle, the dragon and the bear.

Not only does God address His words of truth to those who are able to receive them, He actually conceals their meaning from those who are not. The preacher uses stories to make truth clear; our Lord often used them to obscure it. The parables of Christ were the exact opposite of the modern "illustration," which is meant to give light; the parables were "dark sayings" and Christ asserted that He sometimes used them so that His disciples could understand and His enemies could not. (See Matthew 13:10-17.) As the pillar of fire gave light to Israel but was cloud and darkness to the Egyptians, so our Lord's words shine in the hearts of His people but leave the self-confident unbeliever in the obscurity of moral night.

The saving power of the Word is reserved for those for whom it is intended. The secret of the Lord is with them that fear Him. The impenitent heart will find the Bible but a skeleton of facts without flesh or life or breath. Shakespeare may be enjoyed without penitence; we may understand Plato without believing a word he says; but penitence and humility along with faith and obedience are necessary to a right understanding of the Scriptures.

In natural matters faith follows evidence and is impossible without it, but in the realm of the spirit faith precedes understanding; it does not follow it. The natural man must know in order to believe; the spiritual man must believe in order to know. The faith that saves is not a conclusion drawn from evidence; it is a moral thing, a thing of the spirit, a supernatural infusion of confidence in Jesus Christ, a very gift of God.

The faith that saves reposes in the Person of Christ; it leads at once to a committal of the total being to Christ, an act impossible to the natural man. To believe rightly is as much a miracle as was the coming forth of dead Lazarus at the command of Christ.

The Bible is a supernatural book and can be understood only by supernatural aid.

7
FAITH: THE MISUNDERSTOOD DOCTRINE

In the divine scheme of salvation the doctrine of faith is central. God addresses His words to faith, and where no faith is, no true revelation is possible. "Without faith it is impossible to please him."

Every benefit flowing from the atonement of Christ comes to the individual through the gateway of faith. Forgiveness, cleansing, regeneration, the Holy Spirit, all answers to prayer, are given to faith and received by faith. There is no other way. This is common evangelical doctrine and is accepted wherever the cross of Christ is understood.

Because faith is so vital to all our hopes, so necessary to the fulfillment of every aspiration of our hearts, we dare take nothing for granted concerning it. Anything that carries with it so much of weal or woe, which indeed decides our heaven or our hell, is too important to neglect. We simply must not allow ourselves to be uninformed or misinformed. We must know.

For a number of years my heart has been troubled over the doctrine of faith as it is received and taught among evangelical Christians everywhere. Great emphasis is laid upon faith in orthodox circles, and that is good; but still I am troubled. Specifically, my fear is that the modern conception of faith is not the Biblical one; that when the teachers of our day use the word they do not mean what Bible writers meant when they used it.

The causes of my uneasiness are these:

1. The lack of spiritual fruit in the lives of so many who claim to have faith.

2. The rarity of a radical change in the conduct and general outlook

of persons professing their new faith in Christ as their personal Saviour.

3. The failure of our teachers to define or even describe the thing to which the word faith is supposed to refer.

4. The heartbreaking failure of multitudes of seekers, be they ever so earnest, to make anything out of the doctrine or to receive any satisfying experience through it.

5. The real danger that a doctrine that is parroted so widely and received so uncritically by so many is false as understood by them.

6. I have seen faith put forward as a substitute for obedience, an escape from reality, a refuge from the necessity of hard thinking, a hiding place for weak character. I have known people to miscall by the name of faith high animal spirits, natural optimism, emotional thrills and nervous tics.

7. Plain horse sense ought to tell us that anything that makes no change in the man who professes it makes no difference to God either, and it is an easily observable fact that for countless numbers of persons the change from no-faith to faith makes no actual difference in the life.

Perhaps it will help us to know what faith is if we first notice what it is not. It is not the 'believing' of a statement we know to be true. The human mind is so constructed that it must of necessity believe when the evidence presented to it is convincing. It cannot help itself. When the evidence fails to convince, no faith is possible. No threats, no punishment, can compel the mind to believe against clear evidence.

Faith based upon reason is faith of a kind, it is true; but it is not of the character of Bible faith, for it follows the evidence infallibly and has nothing of a moral or spiritual nature in it. Neither can the absence of faith based upon reason be held against anyone, for the evidence, not the individual, decides the verdict. To send a man to hell whose only crime was to follow evidence straight to its proper conclusion would be palpable injustice; to justify a sinner on the grounds that he had made up his mind according to the plain facts would be to make salvation the result of the workings of a common law of the mind as applicable to Judas as to Paul. It would take salvation out of the realm of the volitional and place it in the mental, where, according to the Scriptures, it surely does not belong.

True faith rests upon the character of God and asks no further proof than the moral perfections of the One who cannot lie. It is enough that God said it, and if the statement should contradict every one of the five senses and all the conclusions of logic as well, still the believer contin-ues to believe. "Let God be true, but every man a liar," is the language of true faith. Heaven approves such faith because it rises above mere proofs and rests in the bosom of God.

In recent years among certain evangelicals there has arisen a move-ment designed to prove the truths of Scriptures by appeal to science. Ev-idence is sought in the natural world to support supernatural revelation. Snowflakes, blood, stones, strange marine creatures, birds and many other natural objects are brought forward as proof that the Bible is true. This is touted as being a great support to faith, the idea being that if a Bible doctrine can be proved to be true, faith will spring up and flourish as a consequence.

What these brethren do not see is that the very fact that they feel a necessity to seek proof for the truths of the Scriptures proves something else altogether, namely, their own basic unbelief. When God speaks un-belief asks, "How shall I know that this is true?" I AM THAT I AM is the only grounds for faith. To dig among the rocks or search under the sea for evidence to support the Scriptures is to insult the One who wrote them. Certainly I do not believe that this is done intentionally; but I can-not see how we can escape the conclusion that it is done, nevertheless.

Faith as the Bible knows it is confidence in God and His Son Jesus Christ; it is the response of the soul to the divine character as revealed in the Scriptures; and even this response is impossible apart from the prior inworking of the Holy Spirit. Faith is a gift of God to a penitent soul and has nothing whatsoever to do with the senses or the data they afford. Faith is a miracle; it is the ability God gives to trust His Son, and anything that does not result in action in accord with the will of God is not faith but something else short of it.

Faith and morals are two sides of the same coin. Indeed the very es-sence of faith is moral. Any professed faith in Christ as personal Saviour that does not bring the life under plenary obedience to Christ as Lord is inadequate and must betray its victim at the last.

The man that believes will obey; failure to obey is convincing proof that there is not true faith present. To attempt the impossible God must give faith or there will be none, and He gives faith to the obedient heart only. Where real repentance is, there is obedience; for repentance is not only sorrow for past failures and sins, it is a determination to begin now to do the will of God as He reveals it to us.

8

TRUE RELIGION IS NOT FEELING BUT WILLING

One of the puzzling questions likely to turn up sooner or later to vex the seeking Christian is how he can fulfill the scriptural command to love God with all his heart and his neighbor as himself.

The earnest Christian, as he meditates on his sacred obligation to love God and mankind, may experience a sense of frustration gendered by the knowledge that he just cannot seem to work up any emotional thrill over his Lord or his brothers. He wants to, but he cannot. The delightful wells of feeling simply will not flow.

Many honest persons have become discouraged by the absence of religious emotion and concluded that they are not really Christian after all. They conclude that they must have missed the way somewhere back there and their religion is little more than an empty profession. So for a while they belabor themselves for their coldness and finally settle into a state of dull discouragement, hardly knowing what to think. They do believe in God; they do indeed trust Christ as their Saviour, but the love they hoped to feel consistently eludes them. What is the trouble?

The problem is not a light one. A real difficulty is involved, one which may be stated in the form of a question: How can I love by commandment? Of all the emotions of which the soul is capable, love is by far the freest, the most unreasoning, the one least likely to spring up at the call of duty or obligation, and surely the one that will not come at the command of another. No law has ever been passed that can compel one moral being to love another, for by the very nature of it love must be voluntary. No one can be coerced or frightened into loving anyone. Love just does not come that way. So what are we to do with our Lord's command to love God and our neighbor?

To find our way out of the shadows and into the cheerful sunlight we need only to know that there are two kinds of love: the love of feeling and the love of willing. The one lies in the emotions, the other in the will. Over the one we may have little control. It comes and goes, rises and falls, flares up and disappears as it chooses, and changes from hot to warm to cool and back to warm again very much as does the weather. Such love was not in the mind of Christ when He told His people to love God and each other. As well command a butterfly to light on our shoulder as to attempt to command this whimsical kind of affection to visit our hearts.

The love the Bible enjoins is not the love of feeling; it is the love of willing, the willed tendency of the heart. (For these two happy phrases I am indebted to another, a master of the inner life whose pen was only a short time ago stilled by death.)

God never intended that such a being as man should be the plaything of his feelings. The emotional life is a proper and noble part of the total personality, but it is, by its very nature, of secondary importance. Religion lies in the will, and so does righteousness. The only good that God recognizes is a willed good; the only valid holiness is a willed holiness.

It should be a cheering thought that before God every man is what he wills to be. The first requirement in conversion is a rectified will. "If any man will," says our Lord, and leaves it there. To meet the requirements of love toward God the soul need but will to love and the miracle begins to blossom like the budding of Aaron's rod.

The will is the automatic pilot that keeps the soul on course. "Flying is easy," said a friend who flies his own plane. "Just take her up, point her in the direction you want her to go and set the pilot. After that she'll fly herself." While we must not press the figure too far, it is yet blessedly true that the will, not the feelings, determines moral direction.

The root of all evil in human nature is the corruption of the will. The thoughts and intents of the heart are wrong and as a consequence the whole life is wrong. Repentance is primarily a change of moral purpose, a sudden and often violent reversal of the soul's direction. The prodigal son took his first step upward from the pigsty when he said, "I will arise and go to my father." As he had once willed to leave his father's house, now he willed to return. His subsequent action proved his expressed purpose to be sincere. He did return.

Someone may infer from the above that we are ruling out the joy of the Lord as a valid part of the Christian life. While no one who reads these columns regularly would be likely to draw such an erroneous conclusion, a chance reader might be led astray; a further word of explanation is therefore indicated:

To love God with all our heart we must first of all will to do so. We should repent our lack of love and determine from this moment on to make God the object of our devotion. We should set our affections on things above and aim our hearts toward Christ and heavenly things. We should read the Scriptures devotionally every day and prayerfully obey them, always firmly willing to love God with all our heart and our neighbor as ourself.

If we do these things we may be sure that we shall experience a wonderful change in our whole inward life. We shall soon find to our great delight that our feelings are becoming less erratic and are beginning to move in the direction of the "willed tendency of the heart." Our emotions will become disciplined and directed. We shall begin to taste the "piercing sweetness" of the love of Christ. Our religious affection will begin to mount evenly on steady wings instead of flitting about idly without purpose or intelligent direction. The whole life, like a delicate instrument, will be tuned to sing the praises of Him who loved us and washed us from our sins in His own blood.

But first of all we must will, for the will is master of the heart.

9

HOW TO MAKE SPIRITUAL PROGRESS

The complacency of Christians is the scandal of Christianity.

Time is short, and eternity is long. The end of all things is at hand. Man has proved himself morally unfit to manage the world in which he has been placed by the kindness of the Almighty. He has jockeyed himself to the edge of the crater and cannot go back, and in terrible fear he is holding his breath against the awful moment when he will be plunged into the inferno.

In the meantime, a company of people exist on the earth who claim to have the answer to all life's major questions. They claim to have found the way back to God, release from their sins, life everlasting and a sure guarantee of heaven in the world to come.

These are the Christians. They declare that Jesus Christ is very God of very God, made flesh to dwell among us. Thy insist that He is the Way, the Truth and the Life. They testify that He is to them Wisdom, Righteousness, Sanctification and Redemption, and they steadfastly assert that He will be to them the Resurrection and the Life for eternity to come.

These Christians know, and when pressed will admit, that their finite hearts have explored but a pitifully small part of the infinite riches that are theirs in Christ Jesus. They read the lives of the great saints whose fervent desire after God carried them far up the mountain toward spiritual perfection; and for a brief moment they may yearn to be like these fiery souls whose light and fragrance still linger in the world where they once lived and labored. But the longing soon passes. The world is too much with them and the claims of their earthly lives are too insistent; so they settle back to live their ordinary lives, and accept the customary as normal. After a while they manage to achieve some kind of inner content and that is the last we hear of them.

This contentment with inadequate and imperfect progress in the life of holiness is, I repeat, a scandal in the Church of the Firstborn. The whole weight of Scripture is against such a thing. The Holy Spirit constantly seeks to arouse the complacent. "Let us go on" is the word of the Spirit. The Apostle Paul embodies this in his noble testimony as found in his Philippian epistle: "But what things were gain to me, those I counted loss for Christ. Yea doubtless, and I count all things but loss for the excellency of the knowledge of Christ Jesus my Lord: for whom I have suffered the loss of all things, and do count them but dung, that I may win Christ . . . that I may know him, and the power of his resurrection . . . but this one thing I do, forgetting those things which are behind, and reaching forth unto those things which are before, I press toward the mark for the prize of the high calling of God in Christ Jesus."

If we accept this as the sincere expression of a normal Christian I do not see how we can justify our own indifference toward spiritual things. But should someone feel a desire to make definite progress in the life of Christ, what can he do to get on with it? Here are a few suggestions:

1. Strive to get beyond mere pensive longing. Set your face like a flint and begin to put your life in order. Every man is as holy as he really wants to be. But the want must be all-compelling.

Tie up the loose ends of your life. Begin to tithe; institute family prayer; pay up your debts as far as possible and make some kind of frank arrangement with every creditor you cannot pay immediately; make restitution as far as you can; set aside time to pray and search the Scriptures; surrender wholly to the will of God. You will be surprised and delighted with the results.

2. Put away every un-Christian habit from you. If other Christians practice it without compunction, God may be calling you to come nearer to Him than these other Christians care to come. Remember the words, "Others may, you cannot." Do not condemn or criticize, but seek a better way. God will honor you.

3. Get Christ Himself in the focus of your heart and keep Him there continually. Only in Christ will you find complete fulfillment. In Him you may be united to the Godhead in conscious, vital awareness. Remember that all of God is accessible to you through Christ. Cultivate

His knowledge above everything else on earth.

4. Throw your heart open to the Holy Spirit and invite Him to fill you. He will do it. Let no one interpret the Scriptures for you in such a way as to rule out the Father's gift of the Spirit. Every man is as full of the Spirit as he wants to be. Make your heart a vacuum and the Spirit will rush in to fill it.

Nowhere in the Scriptures nor in Christian biography was anyone ever filled with the Spirit who did not know that he had been, and nowhere was anyone filled who did not know when. And no one was ever filled gradually.

5. Be hard on yourself and easy on others. Carry your own cross but never lay one on the back of another. Begin to practice the presence of God. Cultivate the fellowship of the Triune God by prayer, humility, obedience and self-abnegation.

Let any Christian do these things and he will make rapid spiritual progress. There is every reason why we should all go forward in our Christian lives and no reason why we should not. Let us go on.

10
THE OLD CROSS AND THE NEW

All unannounced and mostly undetected there has come in modern times a new cross into popular evangelical circles. It is like the old cross, but different: the likenesses are superficial; the differences, fundamental.

From this new cross has sprung a new philosophy of the Christian life, and from that new philosophy has come a new evangelical technique-a new type of meeting and a new kind of preaching. This new evangelism employs the same language as the old, but its content is not the same and its emphasis not as before.

The old cross would have no truck with the world. For Adam's proud flesh it meant the end of the journey. It carried into effect the sentence imposed by the law of Sinai. The new cross is not opposed to the human race; rather, it is a friendly pal and, if understood aright, it is the source of oceans of good clean fun and innocent enjoyment. It lets Adam live without interference. His life motivation is unchanged; he still lives for his own pleasure, only now he takes delight in singing choruses and watching religious movies instead of singing bawdy songs and drinking hard liquor. The accent is still on enjoyment, though the fun is now on a higher plane morally if not intellectually.

The new cross encourages a new and entirely different evangelistic approach. The evangelist does not demand abnegation of the old life before a new life can be received. He preaches not contrasts but similarities. He seeks to key into public interest by showing that Christianity makes no unpleasant demands; rather, it offers the same thing the world does, only on a higher level. Whatever the sin-mad world happens to be clamoring after at the moment is cleverly shown to be the very thing the gospel offers, only the religious product is better.

The new cross does not slay the sinner, it redirects him. It gears him into a cleaner anal jollier way of living and saves his self-respect. To the self-assertive it says, "Come and assert yourself for Christ." To the egotist it says, "Come and do your boasting in the Lord." To the thrillseeker it says, "Come and enjoy the thrill of Christian fellowship." The Christian message is slanted in the direction of the current vogue in order to make it acceptable to the public.

The philosophy back of this kind of thing may be sincere but its sincerity does not save it from being false. It is false because it is blind. It misses completely the whole meaning of the cross.

The old cross is a symbol of death. It stands for the abrupt, violent end of a human being. The man in Roman times who took up his cross and started down the road had already said good-by to his friends. He was not coming back. He was going out to have it ended. The cross made no compromise, modified nothing, spared nothing; it slew all of the man, completely and for good. It did not try to keep on good terms with its victim. It struck cruel and hard, and when it had finished its work, the man was no more.

The race of Adam is under death sentence. There is no commutation and no escape. God cannot approve any of the fruits of sin, however innocent they may appear or beautiful to the eyes of men. God salvages the individual by liquidating him and then raising him again to newness of life.

That evangelism which draws friendly parallels between the ways of God and the ways of men is false to the Bible and cruel to the souls of its hearers. The faith of Christ does not parallel the world, it intersects it. In coming to Christ we do not bring our old life up onto a higher plane; we leave it at the cross. The corn of wheat must fall into the ground and die.

We who preach the gospel must not think of ourselves as public relations agents sent to establish good will between Christ and the world. We must not imagine ourselves commissioned to make Christ acceptable to big business, the press, the world of sports or modern education. We are not diplomats but prophets, and our message is not a compromise but an ultimatum.

God offers life, but not an improved old life. The life He offers is life out of death. It stands always on the far side of the cross. Whoever would possess it must pass under the rod. He must repudiate himself and concur in God's just sentence against him.

What does this mean to the individual, the condemned man who would find life in Christ Jesus? How can this theology be translated into life? Simply, he must repent and believe. He must forsake his sins and then go on to forsake himself. Let him cover nothing, defend nothing, excuse nothing. Let him not seek to make terms with God, but let him bow his head before the stroke of God's stern displeasure and acknowledge himself worthy to die.

Having done this let him gaze with simple trust upon the risen Saviour, and from Him will come life and rebirth and cleansing and power. The cross that ended the earthly life of Jesus now puts an end to the sinner; and the power that raised Christ from the dead now raises him to a new life along with Christ.

To any who may object to this or count it merely a narrow and private view of truth, let me say God has set His hallmark of approval upon this message from Paul's day to the present. Whether stated in these exact words or not, this has been the content of all preaching that has brought life and power to the world through the centuries. The mystics, the reformers, the revivalists have put their emphasis here, and signs and wonders and mighty operations of the Holy Ghost gave witness to God's approval.

Dare we, the heirs of such a legacy of power, tamper with the truth? Dare we with our stubby pencils erase the lines of the blueprint or alter the pattern shown us in the Mount? May God forbid. Let us preach the old cross and we will know the old power.

11
THERE IS NO WISDOM IN SIN

The world has divided men into two classes, the stupid good people and the clever wicked ones.

This false classification runs through much of the literature of the last centuries from the classics to the comic strip, from Shakespeare's Polomus, who furnished his son with a set of good but dull moral platitudes, to Capp's Li'l Abner, who would never knowingly do a wrong act but who would rather fall on his head than on his feet because there is more feeling in his feet than in his head.

In the Holy Scriptures things are quite the opposite. There righteousness is always associated with wisdom and evil with folly. Whatever other factors may be present in an act of wrongdoing, folly is one that is never absent. To do a wrong act a man must for the moment think wrong; he must exercise bad judgment.

If this is true then the devil is creation's prime fool, for when he gambled on his ability to unseat the Almighty he was guilty of an act of judgment so bad as to be imbecilic, He is said to have had a great amount of wisdom, but his wisdom must have deserted him at the time of his first sin, for surely he grossly underestimated the power of God and as grossly overestimated his own. The devil is not now pictured in the Scriptures as wise, only as shrewd. We are warned not against his wisdom but against his wiles, something very different.

Sin, I repeat, in addition to anything else it may be, is always an act of wrong judgment. To commit a sin a man must for the moment believe that things are different from what they really are; he must confound values; he must see the moral universe out of focus; he must accept a lie as truth and see truth as a lie; he must ignore the signs on the highway and drive with his eyes shut; he must act as if he had no soul and was not accountable for his moral choices.

Sin is never a thing to be proud of. No act is wise that ignores remote consequences, and sin always does. Sin sees only today, or at most tomorrow; never the day after tomorrow, next month or next year. Death and judgment are pushed aside as if they did not exist and the sinner becomes for the time a practical atheist who by his act denies not only the existence of God but the concept of life after death.

History is replete with examples of men whose intellectual powers were great but whose practical judgment was almost nil: Einstein, for instance, who was a mathematical genius but who could not look after his own bank account and who absentmindedly ran his little motorboat aground with the excuse that he "must have been thinking about something else." We can smile at this, but there is nothing humorous about that other class of men who had brilliant minds but whose moral judgment was sadly awry. To this class belong such men as Lucretius, Voltaire, Shelley, Oscar Wilde, Walt Whitman and thousands of others whose names are less widely known.

The notion that the careless sinner is the smart fellow and the serious-minded Christian, though well-intentioned, is a stupid dolt altogether out of touch with life will not stand up under scrutiny. Sin is basically an act of moral folly, and the greater the folly the greater the fool.

It is time the young people of this generation learned that there is nothing smart about wrongdoing and nothing stupid about righteousness. We must stop negotiating with evil. We Christians must stop apologizing for our moral position and start making our voices heard, exposing sin for the enemy of the human race which it surely is, and setting forth righteousness and true holiness as the only worthy pursuits for moral beings.

The idea that sin is modern is false. There has not been a new sin invented since the beginning of recorded history. That new vice breaks out to horrify decent citizens and worry the police is not really new. Flip open that book written centuries ago and you will find it described there. The reckless sinner trying to think of some new way to express his love of iniquity can do no more than imitate others like himself, now long dead. He is not the bright rebel he fancies himself to be but a weak and stupid fellow who must follow along in the long parade of death toward the point of no return.

If the hoary head is a crown of glory when it is found in the way of righteousness, it is a fool's cap when it is found in the way of sin. An old sinner is an awesome and frightening spectacle. One feels about him much as one feels about the condemned man on his way to the gallows. A sense of numb terror and shock fills the heart. The knowledge that the condemned man was once a redcheeked boy only heightens the feeling, and the knowledge that the aged rebel now beyond reclamation once went up to the house of God on a Sunday morning to the sweet sound of church bells makes even the trusting Christian humble and a little bit scared. There but for the grace of God goes he.

I am among those who believe that our Western civilization is on its way to perishing. It has many commendable qualities, most of which it has borrowed from the Christian ethic, but it lacks the element of moral wisdom that would give it permanence. Future historians will record that we of the twentieth century had intelligence enough to create a great civilization but not the moral wisdom to preserve it.

12
THREE DEGREES OF RELIGIOUS KNOWLEDGE

In our knowledge of divine things three degrees may be distinguished: the knowledge furnished by reason, by faith and by spiritual experience respectively.

These three degrees of knowledge correspond to the departments of the tabernacle in the ancient Levitical order: the outer court, the holy place and the holy of holies.

Far in, beyond the "second veil," was the holiest of all, having as its lone piece of furniture the Ark of the Covenant with the cherubim of glory shadowing the mercy seat. There between the outstretched wings dwelt in awesome splendor the fire of God's presence, the Shekmah. No light of nature reached that sacred place, only the pure radiance of Him who is light and in whom there is no darkness at all. To that solemn Presence no one could approach except the high priest once each year with blood of atonement.

Farther out, and separated by a heavy veil, was the holy place, a sacred place indeed but removed from the Presence and always accessible to the priests of Israel. Here also the light of sun and moon was excluded; light was furnished by the shining of the seven golden candlesticks.

The court of the priests was out farther still, a large enclosure in which were the brazen altar and the lavar. This was open to the sky and received the normal light of nature.

All was of God and all was divine, but the quality of the worshipper's knowledge became surer and more sublime as he moved in from the outer court toward the mercy seat and the Presence, where at last he was permitted to gaze upon the cherubim of glory and the deep burning

Fire that glowed between their outstretched wings.

All this illustrates if it does not typify the three degrees of knowledge possible to a Christian. It is not proper that we should press every detail in an effort to find in the beautiful Old Testament picture more than is actually there; but the most cautious expositor could hardly object to our using the earthly and external to throw into relief the internal and the heavenly.

Nature is a great teacher and at her feet we may learn much that is good and ennobling. The Bible itself teaches this: "The heavens declare the glory of God; and the firmament showeth his handywork. Day unto day uttereth speech, and night unto night showeth knowledge." "Go to the ant, thou sluggard; consider her ways, and be wise." "Behold the fowls of the air." "For the invisible things of him from the creation of the world are clearly seen, being understood by the things that are made, even his eternal power and Godhead." Reason working on data furnished by observation of natural objects tells us a lot about God and spiritual things. This is too obvious to require proof. Everyone knows it.

But there is knowledge beyond and above that furnished by observation; it is knowledge received by faith. "In religion faith plays the part by experience in the things of the world." Divine revelation through the inspired Scriptures offers data which lie altogether outside of and above the power of the mind to discover. The mind can make its deductions after it has received these data by faith, but it cannot find them by itself. No technique is known to man by which he can learn, for instance, that God in the beginning created the heaven and the earth or that there are three Persons in the Godhead; that God is love or that Christ died for sinners, or that He now sits at the right hand of the Majesty in the heavens. If we ever come to know these things it must be by receiving as true a body of doctrine which we have no way of verifying. This is the knowledge of faith.

There is yet a purer knowledge than this; it is knowledge by direct spiritual experience. About it there is an immediacy that places it beyond doubt. Since it was not acquired by reason operating on intellectual data, the possibility of error is eliminated. Through the indwelling Spirit the human spirit is brought into immediate contact with higher spiritual reality. It looks upon, tastes, feels and sees the powers of the world to come and has a conscious encounter with God invisible.

Let it be understood that such knowledge is experienced rather than acquired. It does not consist of findings about something; it is the thing itself. It is not a compound of religious truths. It is an element which cannot be separated into parts. One who enjoys this kind of knowledge is able to understand the exhortation in the Book of Job: "Acquaint now thyself with him, and be at peace." To such a man God is not a conclusion drawn from evidence nor is He the sum of what the Bible teaches about Him. He knows God in the last irreducible meaning of the word know. It may almost be said that God happened to him.

Maybe Christ said all this more simply in John 14:21: "I . . . will manifest myself to him." For what have we been laboring here but the sublimely simple New Testament teaching that the Triune God wills to dwell in the redeemed man's heart, constantly making His presence known? What on earth or in heaven above can be a greater beatitude?

13
THE SANCTIFICATION OF THE SECULAR

The New Testament teaches that all things are pure to the pure, and I think we may assume that to the evil man all things are evil. The thing itself is not good or bad; goodness or badness belongs to human personality.

Everything depends upon the state of our interior lives and our heart's relation to God. The man that walks with God will see and know that for him there is no strict line separating the sacred from the secular. He will acknowledge that there lies around him a world of created things that are innocent in themselves; and he will know, too, that there are a thousand human acts that are neither good nor bad except as they may be done by good or bad men. The busy world around us is filled with work, travel, marrying, rearing our young, burying our dead, buying, selling, sleeping, eating and mixing in common social intercourse with our fellowmen.

These activities and all else that goes to fill up our days are usually separated in our minds from prayer, church attendance and such specific religious acts as are performed by ministers most of the week and by laymen briefly once or twice weekly.

Because the vast majority of men engage in the complicated business of living while trusting wholly in themselves, without reference to God or redemption, we Christians have come to call these common activities "secular" and to attribute to them at least a degree of evil, an evil which is not inherent in them and which they do not necessarily possess.

The Apostle Paul teaches that every simple act of our lives may be sacramental. "Whether therefore ye eat, or drink, or whatsoever ye do, do all to the glory of God." And again, "Whatsoever ye do in word or deed, do all in the name of the Lord Jesus, giving thanks to God and the Father by him."

Some of the great saints, who were great because they took such admonitions seriously and sought to practice them, managed to achieve the sanctification of the secular, or perhaps I should say the abolition of the secular. Their attitude toward life's common things raised those above the common and imparted to them an aura of divinity. These pure souls broke down the high walls that separated the various areas of their lives from each other and saw all as one; and that one they offered to God as a holy oblation acceptable to God by Jesus Christ.

Nicholas Herman (Brother Lawrence) made his most common act one of devotion: "The time of business does not with me differ from the time of prayer," he said, "and in the noise and clatter of my kitchen, while several persons are at the same time calling for different things, I possess God in as great tranquility as if I were upon my knees at the blessed sacrament."

Francis of Assisi accepted the whole creation as his house of worship and called upon everything great and small to join him in adoration of the Godhead. Mother earth, the burning sun, the silver moon, the stars of evening, wind, water, flowers, fruits-all were invited to praise with him their God and King. Hardly a spot was left that could be called secular. The whole world glowed like Moses' bush with the light of God, and before it the saint kneeled and removed his shoes.

Thomas Traherne, the seventeenth century Christian writer, declared that the children of the King can never enjoy the world aright till every morning they wake up in heaven, see themselves in the Father's palace, and look upon the skies, the earth and the air as celestial joys, having such a reverent esteem for all as if they were among the angels.

All this is not to ignore the fall of man nor to deny the presence of sin in the world. No believing man can deny the Fall, as no observing man can deny the reality of sin; and as far as I know no responsible thinker has ever held that sin could ever be made other than sinful, whether by prayer or faith or spiritual ministrations. Neither the inspired writers of Holy Scripture nor those illuminated souls who have based their teachings upon those Scriptures have tried to make sin other than exceedingly sinful. It is possible to recognize the sacredness of all things even while admitting that for the time the mystery of sin worketh in the children of disobedience and the whole creation groaneth and travaileth, waiting for the manifestation of the children of God.

Traherne saw the apparent contradiction and explained it: "To contemn the world and to enjoy the world are things contrary to each other. How can we contemn the world, which we are born to enjoy? Truly there are two worlds. One was made by God, and the other by men. That made by God was great and beautiful. Before the Fall it was Adam's joy and the temple of his glory. That made by men is a Babel of confusions: invented riches, pomps and vanities, brought in by sin. Give all (saith Thomas a Kempis) for all. Leave the one that you may enjoy the other."

Such souls as these achieved the sanctification of the secular. The church today is suffering from the secularization of the sacred. By accepting the world's values, thinking its thoughts and adopting its ways we have dimmed the glory that shines overhead. We have not been able to bring earth to the judgment of heaven so we have brought heaven to the judgment of the earth. Pity us, Lord, for we know not what we do!

14
GOD MUST BE LOVED FOR HIMSELF

God being who he is must always be sought for Himself, never as a means toward something else.

Whoever seeks other objects and not God is on his own; he may obtain those objects if he is able, but he will never have God. God is never found accidentally. "Ye shall seek me, and find me, when ye shall search for me with all your heart" (Jer. 29:13) .

Whoever seeks God as a means toward desired ends will not find God. The mighty God, the maker of heaven and earth, will not be one of many treasures, not even the chief of all treasures. He will be all in all or He will be nothing. God will not be used. His mercy and grace are infinite and His patient understanding is beyond measure, but He will not aid men in their selfish striving after personal gain. He will not help men to attain ends which, when attained, usurp the place He by every right should hold in their interest and affection.

Yet popular Christianity has as one of its most effective talking points the idea that God exists to help people to get ahead in this world. The God of the poor has become the God of an affluent society. Christ no longer refuses to be a judge or a divider between money hungry brothers. He can now be persuaded to assist the brother that has accepted Him to get the better of the brother who has not.

A crass example of the modern effort to use God for selfish purposes is the well-known comedian who, after repeated failures, promised someone he called God that if He would help him to make good in the entertainment world he would repay Him by giving generously to the care of sick children. Shortly afterward he hit the big time in the night clubs and on television. He has kept his word and is raising large sums of money to build children's hospitals. These contributions to charity, he feels, are a small price to pay for a success in one of the sleaziest fields of human endeavor.

One might excuse the act of this entertainer as something to be expected of a twentieth century pagan; but that multitudes of evangelicals in North America should actually believe that God had anything to do with the whole business is not so easily overlooked. This low and false view of Deity is one major reason for the immense popularity God enjoys these days among well-fed Westerners.

The teaching of the Bible is that God is Himself the end for which man was created. "Whom have I in heaven but thee?" cried the psalmist, "and there is none upon earth that I desire beside thee" (Psa. 73: 25) . The first and greatest commandment is to love God with every power of our entire being. Where love like that exists there can be no place for a second object. If we love God as much as we should surely we cannot dream of a loved object beyond Him which He might help us to obtain.

Bernard of Clairvaux begins his radiant little treatise on the love of God with a question and an answer. The question, Why should we love God? The answer, Because He is God. He develops the idea further, but for the enlightened heart little more need be said. We should love God because He is God. Beyond this the angels cannot think.

Being who He is, God is to be loved for His own sake. He is the reason for our loving Him, just as He is the reason for His loving us and for every other act He has performed, is performing and will perform world without end. God's primary reason for everything is His own good pleasure. The search for secondary reasons is gratuitous and mostly futile. It affords occupation for theologians and adds pages to books on doctrine, but that it ever turns up any true explanations is doubtful.

But it is the nature of God to share. His mighty acts of creation and redemption were done for His good pleasure, but His pleasure extends to all created things. One has but to look at a healthy child at play or listen to the song of a bird at sundown and he will know that God meant His universe to be a joyful one.

Those who have been spiritually enabled to love God for Himself will find a thousand fountains springing up from the rainbowcircled throne and bringing countless treasures which are to be received with reverent thanksgiving as being the overflow of God's love for His children. Each gift is a bonus of grace which because it was not sought for itself may be enjoyed without injury to the soul. These include the simple blessings of life, such as health, a home, a family, congenial friends, food, shelter, the pure joys of nature or the more artificial pleasures of music and art.

The effort to find these treasures by direct search apart from God has been the major activity of mankind through the centuries; and this has been man's burden and man's woe. The effort to gain them as the ulterior motive back of accepting Christ may be something new under the sun; but new or old it is an evil that can only bring judgment at last.

God wills that we should love Him for Himself alone with no hidden reasons, trusting Him to be to us all our natures require. Our Lord said all this much better: "Seek ye first the kingdom of God, and his righteousness; and all these things shall be added unto you" (Matt. 6:33) .

15
TRUE FAITH IS ACTIVE, NOT PASSIVE

A christian is one who believes on Jesus Christ as Lord. With this statement every evangelical agrees. Indeed there would appear to be nothing else to do, since the New Testament is crystal clear about the matter.

This first acknowledgment of Christ as Lord and Saviour is usually followed by baptism and membership in a Protestant church, the one because it satisfies a craving for fellowship with others of like mind. A few Christians shy away from organized religion, but the vast majority, while they recognize the imperfections of the churches, nevertheless feel that they can serve their Lord better in the church than out of it.

There is, however, one serious flaw in all this: it is that manywould I overstate the case if I said the majority?-of those who confess their faith in Christ and enter into association with the community of believers have little joy in their hearts, no peace in their minds, and from all external appearances are no better morally than the ordinary educated citizen who takes no interest whatever in religion and, of course, makes no profession of Christianity. Why is this?

I believe it is the result of an inadequate concept of Christianity and an imperfect understanding of the revolutionary character of Christian discipleship.

Certainly there is nothing new in my conclusion. The evangelists are loud in their lamentation over the bodies of dead church members, as well they might be, and many thoughtful articles and books appear from time to time dealing with the serious hiatus between faith and practice among Christians.

Why then add another feeble voice to the many? Because many who lament the condition do not seem to know what to do about it, and because I believe that the way is plain, if hard, and that there is no excuse for going on at this poor dying rate when we can enjoy abundant life in Christ Jesus. True faith brings a spiritual and moral transformation and an inward witness that cannot be mistaken. These come when we stop believing in belief and start believing in the Lord Jesus Christ indeed.

True faith is not passive but active. It requires that we meet certain conditions, that we allow the teachings of Christ to dominate our total lives from the moment we believe. The man of saving faith must be willing to be different from others. The effort to enjoy the benefits of redemption while enmeshed in the world is futile. We must choose one or the other; and faith quickly makes its choice, one from which there is no retreat.

The change experienced by a truly converted man is equal to that of a man moving to another country. The regenerated soul feels no more at home in the world than Abraham felt when he left Ur of the Chaldees and set out for the land of promise. Apart from his own small company he was a stranger to everyone around him. He was called "Abraham the Hebrew," and if he spoke the language of the people among whom he took up his dwelling place, he spoke it with an accent. They all knew that he was not one of them.

This journey from Ur to Bethel is taken by every soul that sets out to follow Christ. It is. however, not a journey for the feet but for the heart. The newborn Christian is a migrant; he has come into the kingdom of God from his old home in the kingdom of man and he must get set for the violent changes that will inevitably follow.

One of the first changes will be a shift of interest from earth to heaven, from men to God, from time to eternity, from earthly gain to Christ and His eternal kingdom. Suddenly, or slowly but surely, he will develop a new pattern of life. Old things will pass away and behold, all things will become new, first inwardly and then outwardly; for the change within him will soon begin to express itself by corresponding changes in his manner of living.

The transformation will show itself in many ways and his former friends will begin to worry about him. At first they will tease him and then chide him; and if he persists in his determination to follow Christ they may begin to oppose and persecute. The onceborn never understand the twice-born, and still after thousands of years Cain hates Abel and Esau threatens Jacob. It is as true today as it was in Bible times that the man who hates his sins too much will get into trouble with those who do not hate sin enough. People resent having their friends turn away from them and by implication condemn their way of life.

The change will reveal itself further in what the new Christian reads, in the places he goes and the friends he cultivates, what he does with his time and how he spends his money. Indeed faith leaves no area of the new believer's life unaffected.

The genuinely renewed man will have a new life center. He will experience a new orientation affecting his whole personality. He will become aware of a different philosophic outlook. Things he once held to be of value may suddenly lose all their attraction for him and he may even hate some things he formerly loved.

The man who recoils from this revolutionary kind of Christianity is retreating before the cross. But thousands do so retreat, and they try to make things right by seeking baptism and church membership. No wonder they are so dissatisfied.

16
ON TAKING TOO MUCH FOR GRANTED

O nce Mary and Joseph, with a number of friends and relatives, were traveling back home from Jerusalem and, supposing the young Jesus to be in the company, went a whole day's journey before discovering that He had been left behind.

Their fault was that they assumed that what they wanted to believe was so in fact. They took too much for granted. A simple check at the start of the journey would have saved them a harrowing experience of fear and uncertainty and two days' unnecessary travel.

Theirs was a pardonable fault and one that we ourselves are in great danger of committing. The whole company of evangelicals is traveling home supposing things, some of which may not be true. We had better check before we go any further. Our failure to do so could have more serious consequences than those suffered by Mary and Joseph. It could lead straight to tragedy.

There is danger that we take Christ for granted. We "suppose" that because we hold New Testament beliefs we are therefore New Testament Christians; but it does not follow. The devil is a better theologian than any of us and is a devil still.

We may, for instance, assume that salvation is possible without repentance. Pardon without penitence is a delusion which simple honesty requires that we expose for what it is. To be forgiven, a sin must be forsaken. This accords with the Scriptures, with common logic and with the experience of the saints of all ages.

We are also in danger of assuming the value of religion without righteousness. Through the various media of public communication we are being pressured into believing that religion 'is little more than a beautiful thing capable of bringing courage and peace of mind to a troubled world. Let us resist this effort at brainwashing. The purpose of Christ's redeeming work was to make it possible for bad men to become good-deeply, radically and finally. God translates men out of the kingdom of darkness into the kingdom of the Son of His love. To believe that such translated men must still dwell in darkness is a reflection on the blood of Christ and the wisdom of God.

In spite of all that James said to the contrary, we are still likely to take for granted that faith without works does somehow have a mystic value after all. But "faith worketh by love," said Paul, and where the works of love are absent we can only conclude that faith is absent also. Faith in faith has displaced faith in God in too many places.

A whole new generation of Christians has come up believing that it is possible to "accept" Christ without forsaking the world. But what saith the Holy Ghost? "Ye adulterers and adulteresses, know ye not that the friendship of the world is enmity with God? whosoever therefore will be a friend of the world is the enemy of God" (James 4:4), and "If any man love the world, the love of the Father is not in him" (I John 2:15) . This requires no comment, only obedience.

We may also erroneously assume that we can experience justification without transformation. Justification and regeneration are not the same; they may be thought apart in theology but they can never be experienced apart in fact. When God declares a man righteous He instantly sets about to make him righteous. Our error today is that we do not expect a converted man to be a transformed man, and as a result of this error our churches are full of substandard Christians. A revival is among other things a return to the belief that real faith invariably produces holiness of heart and righteousness of life.

Again, we may go astray by assuming that we can do spiritual work without spiritual power. I have heard the notion seriously advanced that whereas once to win men to Christ it was necessary to have a gift from the Holy Spirit, now religious movies make it possible for anyone to win souls, without such spiritual anointing! "Whom the gods would destroy they first make mad." Surely such a notion is madness, but until now I have not heard it challenged among the evangelicals.

David Brainerd once compared a man without the power of the Spirit trying to do spiritual work to a workman without fingers attempting to do manual labor. The figure is striking but it does not overstate the facts. The Holy Spirit is not a luxury meant to make deluxe Christians, as an illuminated frontispiece and a leather binding make a deluxe book. The Spirit is an imperative necessity. Only the Eternal Spirit can do eternal deeds.

Without exhausting the list of things wrongly taken for granted I would mention one more: Millions take for granted that it is possible to live for Christ without first having died with Christ. This is a serious error and we dare not leave it unchallenged.

The victorious Christian has known two lives. The first was his life in Adam which was motivated by the carnal mind and can never please God in any way. It can never be converted; it can only die (Rom. 8:5-8).

The second life of the Christian is his new life in Christ (Rom. 6:114). To live a Christian life with the life of Adam is wholly impossible. Yet multitudes take for granted that it can be done and go on year after year in defeat. And worst of all they accept this half-dead condition as normal.

For our own soul's sake, let's not take too much for granted.

17
THE CURE FOR A FRETFUL SPIRIT

The Holy Spirit in Psalm 37 admonishes us to beware of irritation in our religious lives:

"Fret not thyself because of evildoers, neither be thou envious against the workers of iniquity."

The word "fret" comes to us from the Anglo-Saxon and carries with it such a variety of meanings as bring a rather pained smile to our faces. Notice how they expose us and locate us behind our disguises. The primary meaning of the word is to eat, and from there it has been extended with rare honesty to cover most of the manifestations of an irritable disposition. "To eat away; to gnaw; to chafe; to gall; to vex; to worry; to agitate; to wear away"; so says Webster, and all who have felt the exhausting, corrosive effects of fretfulness know how accurately the description fits the facts.

Now, the grace of God in the human heart works to calm the agitation that normally accompanies life in such a world as ours. The Holy Spirit acts as a lubricant to reduce the friction to a minimum and to stop the fretting and chafing in their grosser phases. But for most of us the problem is not as simple as that.

Fretfulness may be trimmed down to the ground and its roots remain alive deep within the soul, there growing and extending themselves all unsuspected, sending up their old poisonous shoots under other names and other appearances.

It was not to the unregenerate that the words "Fret not" were spoken, but to God-fearing persons capable of understanding spiritual things. We Christians need to watch and pray lest we fall into this temptation and spoil our Christian testimony by an irritable spirit under the stress and strain of life.

It requires great care and a true knowledge of ourselves to distinguish a spiritual burden from religious irritation. We cannot close our minds to everything that is happening around us. We dare not rest at ease in Zion when the church is so desperately in need of spiritually sensitive men and women who can see her faults and try to call her back to the path of righteousness. The prophets and apostles of Bible times carried in their hearts such crushing burdens for God's wayward people that they could say, "Tears have been my meat day and night," and "Oh that my head were waters, and mine eyes a fountain. of tears, that I might weep day and night for the slain daughter of my people!" These men were heavy with a true burden. What they felt was not vexation but acute concern for the honor of God and the souls of men.

By nature some persons fret easily. They have difficulty separating their personal antipathies from the burden of the Spirit. When they are grieved they can hardly say whether it is a pure and charitable thing or merely irritation set up by other Christians having opinions different from their own.

Of one thing we may be sure, we can never escape the external stimuli that cause vexation. The world is full of them and though we were to retreat to a cave and live the remainder of our days alone we still could not lose them. The rough floor of our cave would chafe us, the weather would irritate us and the very silence would cause us to fret.

Deliverance from a fretting spirit may be by blood and fire, by humility, self-abnegation and a patient carrying of the cross. There will always be "evildoers" and "workers of iniquity," and for the most part they will appear to succeed while the forces of righteousness will seem to fail. The wicked will always have the money and the talent and the publicity and the numbers, while the righteous will be few and poor and unknown. The prayerless Christian will surely misread the signs and fret against the circumstances. That is what the Spirit warns us against.

Let us look out calmly upon the world; or better yet, let us look down upon it from above where Christ is seated and we are seated in Him. Though the wicked spread himself like "a green bay tree" it is only for a moment. Soon he passes away and is not. "But the salvation of the righteous is of the Lord: he is their strength in the time of trouble." This knowledge should cure the fretting spirit.

18
BOASTING OR BELITTLING

We all know how painful it is to be forced to listen to a confirmed boaster sound off on his favorite topic - himself. To be the captive of such a man even for a short time tries our patience to the utmost and puts a heavy strain upon our Christian charity.

Boasting is particularly offensive when it is heard among the children of God, the one place above all others where it should never be found. Yet it is quite common among Christians, though disguised somewhat by the use of the stock expression, "I say this to the glory of God."

Some boasters appear to feel a bit self-conscious, and apologize meekly for their outbursts of self-praise. Others have accepted themselves as being all their doting relatives and friends claim they are, and habitually speak of themselves in reverent terms, as if their superiority was a matter of common knowledge too well established to require proof. Such a one was the concert singer who replied to a glowing compliment after a performance, "Well, what did you expect?"

God is very patient with His children and often tolerates in them carnal traits so gross as to shock their fellow Christians. But that is only for a while. As more light comes to our hearts, and especially as we go on to new and advanced spiritual experiences, God begins to impose disciplines upon us to purge us from the same faults He tolerated before. Then He permits us to say and do things that react unfavorably against us and expose our vanity for what it is. It may then happen in the providential will of God that the very gift we have boasted of may be lost to us or the project we are so proud of will fail. After we have learned our lesson the Lord may restore what He has taken away, for He is more concerned with our souls than with our service. But sometimes our boasting permanently hurts us and excludes us from blessings we might have enjoyed.

Another habit not quite so odious is belittling ourselves. This might seem to be the exact opposite of boasting, but actually it is the same old sin traveling under a nom de plume. It is simply egoism trying to act spiritual. It is impatient Saul hastily offering an unacceptable sacrifice to the Lord.

Self-derogation is bad for the reason that self must be there to derogate. Self, whether swaggering or groveling, can never be anything but hateful to God.

Boasting is an evidence that we are pleased with self; belittling, that we are disappointed in it. Either way we reveal that we have a high opinion of ourselves. The belittler is chagrined that one as obviously superior as he should not have done better, and he punishes himself by making uncomplimentary remarks about himself. That he does not really mean what he says may be proved quite easily. Let someone else say the same things. His eager defense of himself will reveal how he feels and has secretly felt all the time.

The victorious Christian neither exalts nor downgrades himself. His interests have shifted from self to Christ. What he is or is not no longer concerns him. He believes that he has been crucified with Christ and he is not willing either to praise or deprecate such a man.

Yet the knowledge that he has been crucified is only half the victory. "Nevertheless I live; yet not I, but Christ liveth in me: and the life which I now live in the flesh I live by the faith of the Son of God, who loved me, and gave himself for me." Christ is now where the man's ego was formerly. The man is now Christ-centered instead of self-centered, and he forgets himself in his delighted preoccupation with Christ.

Candor compels me to acknowledge that it is a lot easier to write about this than it is to live it. Self is one of the toughest plants that grows in the garden of life. It is, in fact, indestructible by any human means. Just when we are sure it is dead it turns up somewhere as robust as ever to trouble our peace and poison the fruit of our lives.

Yet there is deliverance. When our judicial crucifixion becomes actual the victory is near; and when our faith rises to claim the risen life of Christ as our own the triumph is complete. The trouble is that we do not receive the benefits of all this until something radical has happened in our own experience, something which in its psychological effects approaches actual crucifixion. What Christ went through we also must go through. Rejection, surrender, loss, a violent detachment from the world, the pain of social ostracism - all must be felt in our actual experience.

Where we have failed is in the practical application of the teaching concerning the crucified life. Too many have been content to be armchair Christians, satisfied with the theology of the cross. Plainly Christ never intended that we should rest in a mere theory of self-denial. His teaching identified His disciples with Himself so intimately that they would have had to be extremely dull not to have understood that they were expected to experience very much the same pain and loss as He Himself did.

The healthy soul is the victorious soul and victory never comes while self is permitted to remain unjudged and uncrucified. While we boast or belittle we may be perfectly sure that the cross has not yet done its work within us. Faith and obedience will bring the cross into the life and cure both habits.

19

THE COMMUNION OF SAINTS

I believe in the communion of saints.
—Apostles' Creed

These words were written into the creed about the middle of the fifth century.

It would be difficult if not altogether impossible for us at this late date to know exactly what was in the minds of the Church Fathers who introduced the words into the creed, but in the Book of Acts we have a description of the first Christian communion: "Then they that gladly received his word were baptized: and the same day there were added unto them about three thousand souls. And they continued steadfastly in the apostles' doctrine and fellowship, and in breaking of bread, and in prayers."

Here is the original apostolic fellowship, the pattern after which every true Christian communion must be modelled.

The word "fellowship," in spite of its abuses, is still a beautiful and meaningful word. When rightly understood it means the same as the word "communion," that is, the act and condition of sharing together in some common blessing by numbers of persons. The communion of saints, then, means an intimate and loving sharing together of certain spiritual blessings by persons who are on an equal footing before the blessing in which they share. This fellowship must include every member of the Church of God from Pentecost to this present moment and on to the end of the age.

Now, before there can be communion there must be union. The sharers are one in a sense altogether above organization, nationality, race or denomination. That oneness is a divine thing, achieved by the Holy Spirit in the act of regeneration. Whoever is born of God is one with everyone else who is born of God. Just as gold is always gold, wherever and in whatever shape it is found, and every detached scrap of gold belongs to the true family and is composed of the same element, so every regenerate soul belongs to the universal Christian community and to the fellowship of the saints.

Every redeemed soul is born out of the same spiritual life as every other redeemed soul and partakes of the divine nature in exactly the same manner. Each one is thus made a member of the Christian community and a sharer in everything which that community enjoys. This is the true communion of saints. But to know this is not enough. If we would enter into the power of it we must exercise ourselves in this truth; we must practice thinking and praying with the thought that we are members of the Body of Christ and brothers to all the ransomed saints living and dead who have believed on Christ and acknowledged Him as Lord.

We have said that the communion of saints is a fellowship, a sharing in certain divinely given things by divinely called persons. Now, what are those things?

The first and most important is life-"the life of God in the soul of man," to borrow a phrase from Henry Scougal. This life is the basis of everything else which is given and shared. And that life is nothing else than God Himself. It should be evident that there can be no true Christian sharing unless there is first an impartation of life. An organization and a name do not make a church. One hundred religious persons knit into a unity by careful organization do not constitute a church any more than eleven dead men make a football team. The first requisite is life, always.

The apostolic fellowship is also a fellowship of truth. The inclusiveness of the fellowship must always be held along with the exclusiveness of it. Truth brings into its gracious circle all who admit and accept the Bible as the source of all truth and the Son of God as the Saviour of men. But there dare be no weak compromise with the facts, no sentimental mouthing of the old phrases: "We are all headed for the same place .... Each one is seeking in his own way to please the Father and make heaven his home." The truth makes men free, and the truth will bind and loose, will open and shut, will include and exclude at its high will without respect to persons. To reject or deny the truth of the Word is to exclude ourselves from the apostolic communion.

Now, someone may ask, "What is the truth of which you speak? Is my fate to depend upon Baptist truth or Presbyterian truth or Anglican truth, or all of these or none of these? To know the communion of saints must I believe in Calvinism or Armimanism? In the Congregational or the Episcopal form of church government? Must I interpret prophecy in accord with the pre-millenarians or the post-millenarians? Must I believe in immersion or sprinkling or pouring?" The answer to all this is easy. The confusion is only apparent, not actual.

The early Christians, under the fire of persecution, driven from place to place, sometimes deprived of the opportunity for careful instruction in the faith, wanted a "rule" which would sum up all that they must believe to assure their everlasting welfare. Out of this critical need arose the creeds. Of the many, the Apostles' Creed is the best known and best loved, and has been reverently repeated by the largest number of believers through the centuries. And for millions of good men that creed contains the essentials of truth. Not all truths, to be sure, but the heart of all truth. It served in trying days as a kind of secret password that instantly united men to each other when passed from lip to lip by the followers of the Lamb. It is fair to say, then, that the truth shared by saints in the apostolic fellowship is the same truth which is outlined for convenience in the Apostles' Creed.

In this day when the truth of Christianity is under serious fire from so many directions it is most important that we know what we believe and that we guard it carefully. But in our effort to interpret and expound the Holy Scriptures in accord with the ancient faith of all Christians, we should remember that a seeking soul may find salvation through the blood of Christ while yet knowing little of the fuller teachings of Christian theology. We must, therefore, admit to our fellowship every sheep who has heard the voice of the Shepherd and has tried to follow Him.

The beginner in Christ who has not yet had time to learn much Christian truth and the underprivileged believer who has had the misfortune to be brought up in a church where the Word has been neglected from the pulpit, are very much in the same situation. Their faith grasps only a small portion of truth, and their "sharing" is necessarily limited to the small portion they grasp. The important thing, however, is that the little bit they do enjoy is real truth. It may be no more than this, that "Christ Jesus came into the world to save sinners"; but if they walk in the light of that much truth, no more is required to bring them into the circle of the blessed and to constitute them true members of the apostolic fellowship.

Then, true Christian communion consists in the sharing of a Presence. This is not poetry merely, but a fact taught in bold letters in the New Testament.

God has given us Himself in the Person of His Son. "Where two or three are gathered together in my name, there am I in the midst of them." The immanence of God in His universe makes possible the enjoyment of the "real Presence" by the saints of God in heaven and on earth simultaneously. Wherever they may be, He is present to them in the fullness of His Godhead.

I do not believe that the Bible teaches the possibility of communication between the saints on earth and those in heaven. But while there cannot be communication, there most surely can be communion. Death does not tear the individual believer from his place in the Body of Christ. As in our human bodies each member is nourished by the same blood which at once gives life and unity to the entire organism, so in the Body of Christ the quickening Spirit flowing through every part gives life and unity to the whole. Our Christian brethren who have gone from our sight retain still their place in the universal fellowship. The Church is one, whether waking or sleeping, by a unity of life forevermore.

The most important thing about the doctrine of the communion of saints is its practical effects on the lives of Christians. We know very little about the saints above, but about the saints on earth we know, or can know, a great deal. We Protestants do not believe (since the Bible does not teach) that the saints who have gone into heaven before us are in any way affected by the prayers or labors of saints who remain on earth. Our particular care is not for those whom God has already honored with the vision beatific, but for the hard-pressed and struggling pilgrims who are still traveling toward the City of God. We all belong to each other; the spiritual welfare of each one is or should be the loving concern of all the rest.

We should pray for an enlargement of soul to receive into our hearts all of God's people, whatever their race, color or church affiliation. Then we should practice thinking of ourselves as members of the blessed family of God and should strive in prayer to love and appreciate everyone who is born of the Father.

I suggest also that we try to acquaint ourselves as far as possible with the good and saintly souls who lived before our times and now belong to the company of the redeemed in heaven. How sad to limit our sympathies to those of our own day, when God in His providence has made it possible for us to enjoy the rich treasures of the minds and hearts of so many holy and gifted saints of other days. To confine our reading to the works of a few favorite authors of today or last week is to restrict our horizons and to pinch our souls dangerously.

I have no doubt that the prayerful reading of some of the great spiritual classics of the centuries would destroy in us forever that constriction of soul which seems to he the earmark of modern evangelicalism.

For many of us the wells of the past wait to be reopened. Augustine, for instance, would bring to us a sense of the overwhelming majesty of God that would go far to cure the flippancy of spirit found so widely among modern Christians. Bernard of Cluny would sing to us of "Jerusalem the Golden" and the peace of an eternal sabbath day until the miserable pleasures of this world become intolerable; Richard Rolle would show us how to escape from "the abundance of riches, the flattering of women and the fairness of

youth," that we may go on to know God with an intimacy that will become in our hearts "heat, fragrance and song"; Tersteegen would whisper to us of the "hidden love of God" and the awful Presence until our hearts would become "still before Him" and "prostrate inwardly adore Him"; before our eyes the sweet St. Francis would throw his arms of love around sun and moon, trees and rain, bird and beast, and thank God for them all in a pure rapture of spiritual devotion.

But who is able to complete the roster of the saints? To them we owe a debt of gratitude too great to comprehend: prophet and apostle, martyr and reformer, scholar and translator, hymnist and composer, teacher and evangelist, not to mention ten thousand times ten thousand simplehearted and anonymous souls who kept the flame of pure religion alive even in those times when the faith of our fathers was burning but dimly all over the world.

They belong to us, all of them, and we belong to them. They and we and all redeemed men and women of whatever age or clime are included in the universal fellowship of Christ, and together compose "a royal priesthood, an holy nation, a peculiar people," who enjoy a common but blessed communion of saints.

20
TEMPERAMENT IN THE
CHRISTIAN LIFE

A celebrated American preacher once advanced the novel theory that the various denominations with their different doctrinal emphases served a useful purpose as gathering places for persons of similar temperaments. Christians, he suggested, tend to gravitate toward others of like mental types. Hence the denominations.

Undoubtedly this is oversimplification carried to the point of error. There are too many persons of dissimilar temperaments in every denomination to support such a sweeping classification. Yet I believe that we have here an instance where an error may serve to point up a truth, the truth being that temperament has a great deal to do with our religious views and with the emphases we lay on spiritual matters generally.

It may be a bit difficult to determine which is cause and which effect, but I have noticed that historically Calvinism has flourished among peoples of a markedly phlegmatic disposition. While it is true that Jacob Arminius was a Dutchman, on the whole the Dutch people appear temperamentally quite suited to Calvinism. On the other hand, it would be hard to imagine a Calvinistic Spaniard or Italian. Isolated instances there certainly are, but for the most part the buoyant, volatile, mandolin-playing Latin does not take naturally to long periods of meditation on the divine sovereignty and the eternal decrees.

While we all pride ourselves that we draw our beliefs from the Holy Scriptures, along those border lines where good men disagree we may unconsciously take sides with our temperament. Cast of mind may easily determine our views when the Scriptures are not clear.

People may be classified roughly into two psychological types, the gay and the somber, and it is easy to see how each type will be attracted to the doctrinal views that agree most naturally with its own mental cast. The Calvinist, for instance, never permits himself to become too happy, while the Arminian tends to equate gravity of disposition with coldness of heart and tries to cure it with a revival.

No Calvinist could have written the radiant hymns of Bernard of Clairvaux or Charles Wesley. Calvinism never produced a Christian mystic, unless we except John Newton who was near to being a mystic and did write a few hymns almost as radiant as those of Bernard.

To square the records, however, it should be said that if the Calvinist does not rise as high, he usually stays up longer. He places more emphasis on the Holy Scriptures which never change, while his opposite number (as the newspapers say) tends to judge his spiritual condition by the state of his feelings, which change constantly. This may be the reason that so many Calvinistic churches remain orthodox for centuries, at least in doctrine, while many churches of the Arminian persuasion often go liberal in one generation.

I realize that I am doing a bit of oversimplifying on my own here; still I believe there is more than a germ of truth in the whole thing. Anyway, I am less concerned with the effect of temperament on the historic church, which obviously I can do nothing about, than with its effect upon my own soul and the souls of my readers, whom I may be able to influence somewhat.

Whether or not my broader conclusions are sound, there would seem to be no reason to doubt that we naturally tend to interpret Scripture in the light (or shadow) of our own temperament and let our peculiar mental cast decide the degree of importance we attach to various religious doctrines and practices.

The odd thing about this human quirk is that it prospers most where there is the greatest amount of religious freedom. The authoritarian churches that tell their adherents exactly what to believe and where to lay their emphasis produce a fair degree of uniformity among their members. By stretching everyone on the bed of Procrustes they manage to lengthen or trim back the individual temperament to their liking. The free Protestant, who is still permitted a certain amount of private interpretation, is much more likely to fall into the trap of temperament. Exposure to this temptation is one price he pays for his freedom.

The minister above all others should look deep into his own heart to discover the reason for his more pronounced views. It is not enough to draw himself up and declare with dignity that he preaches the Bible find nothing but the Bible. That claim is made by every man who stands in sincerity to declare the truth; but truth has many facets and the man of God is in grave danger of revealing only a limited few to his people, and those the ones he by disposition favors most.

One cannot imagine Francis of Assisi preaching Edward's sermon, "Sinners in the Hands of an Angry God," nor can we picture Jonathan Edwards preaching to the birds or calling upon sun and moon and wind and stars to join him in praising the Lord. Yet both were good men who loved God deeply and trusted Christ completely. Many other factors besides temperament must not be overlooked.

Are we then to accept the bias of disposition as something inevitable? Are we to allow our religious views to be dictated by ancestors long dead whose genes still stir within us? By no means. The Scriptures, critical self-discipline, honesty of heart and increased trust in the inward operations of the Holy Spirit will save us from being too greatly influenced by temperament.

21
DOES GOD ALWAYS ANSWER PRAYER?

Contrary to popular opinion, the cultivation of a psychology of un-critical belief is not an unqualified good, and if carried too far it may be a positive evil. The whole world has been booby-trapped by the devil, and the deadliest trap of all is the religious one. Error never looks so innocent as when it is found in the sanctuary.

One field where harmless-looking but deadly traps appear in great profusion is the field of prayer. There are more sweet notions about prayer than could be contained in a large book, all of them wrong and all highly injurious to the souls of men.

I think of one such false notion that is found often in pleasant places consorting smilingly with other notions of unquestionable orthodoxy. It is that God always answers prayer.

This error appears among the saints as a kind of all-purpose phil-osophic therapy to prevent any disappointed Christian from suffering too great a shock when it becomes evident to him that his prayer expec-tations are not being fulfilled. It is explained that God always answers prayer, either by saying Yes or by saying No, or by substituting some-thing else for the desired favor.

Now, it would be hard to invent a neater trick than this to save face for the petitioner whose requests have been rejected for non-obedience. Thus when a prayer is not answered he has but to smile brightly and ex-plain, "God said No." It is all so very comfortable. His wobbly faith is saved from confusion and his conscience is permitted to lie undisturbed. But I wonder if it is honest.

To receive an answer to prayer as the Bible uses the term and as

Christians have understood it historically, two elements must be. present: (1) A clear-cut request made to God for a specific favor. (2) A clear-cut granting of that favor by God in answer to the request. There must be no semantic twisting, no changing of labels, no altering of the map during the journey to help the embarrassed tourist to find himself.

When we go to God with a request that He modify the existing situation for us, that is, that He answer prayer, there are two conditions that we must meet: (1) We must pray in the will of God and (2) we must be on what old-fashioned Christians often call "praying ground"; that is, we must be living lives pleasing to God.

It is futile to beg God to act contrary to His revealed purposes. To pray with confidence the petitioner must be certain that his request falls within the broad will of God for His people.

The second condition is also vitally important. God has not placed Himself under obligation to honor the requests of worldly, carnal or disobedient Christians. He hears and answers the prayers only of those who walk in His way. "Beloved, if our heart condemn us not, then have we confidence toward God. And whatsoever we ask, we receive of him, because we keep his commandments, and do those things that are pleasing in his sight . . . . If ye abide in me, and my words abide in you, ye shall ask what ye will, and it shall be done unto you" (I John 3:21, 22; John 15:7).

God wants us to pray and He wants to answer our prayers, but He makes our use of prayer as a privilege to commingle with His use of prayer as a discipline. To receive answers to prayer we must meet God's terms. If we neglect His commandments our petitions will not be honored. He will alter situations only at the request of obedient and humble souls.

The God-always-answers-prayer sophistry leaves the praying man without discipline. By the exercise of this bit of smooth casuistry he ignores the necessity to live soberly, righteously and godly in this present world, and actually takes God's flat refusal to answer his prayer as the very answer itself. Of course such a man will not grow in holiness; he will never learn how to wrestle and wait; he will never know correction; he will not hear the voice of God calling him forward; he will never arrive at the place where he is morally and spiritually fit to have his prayers answered. His wrong philosophy has ruined him.

That is why I turn aside to expose the bit of bad theology upon which his bad philosophy is founded. The man who accepts it never knows where he stands; he never knows whether or not he has true faith, for if his request is not granted he avoids the implication by the simple dodge of declaring that God switched the whole thing around and gave him something else. He will not allow himself to shoot at a target, so he cannot tell how good or how bad a marksman he is.

Of certain persons James says plainly: "Ye ask, and receive not, because ye ask amiss, that ye may consume it upon your lusts." From that brief sentence we may learn that God refuses some requests because they who make them are not morally worthy to receive the answer. But this means nothing to the one who has been seduced into the belief that God always answers prayer. When such a man asks and receives not he passes his hand over the hat and comes up with the answer in some other form. One thing he clings to with great tenacity: God never turns anyone away, but invariably grants every request.

The truth is that God always answers the prayer that accords with His will as revealed in the Scriptures, provided the one who prays is obedient and trustful. Further than this we dare not go.

22
SELF-DECEPTION AND HOW TO AVOID IT

Of all forms of deception, self-deception is the most deadly, and of all deceived persons the self-deceived are the least likely to discover the fraud.

The reason for this is simple. When a man is deceived by another he is deceived against his will. He is contending against an adversary and is temporarily the victim of the other's guile. Since he expects his foe to take advantage of him he is watchful and quick to suspect trickery. Under such circumstances it is possible to be deceived sometimes and for a short while, but because the victim is resisting he may break out of the trap and escape before too long.

With the self-deceived it is quite different. He is his own enemy and is working a fraud upon himself. He wants to believe the lie and is psychologically conditioned to do so. He does not resist the deceit but collaborates with it against himself. There is no struggle, because the victim surrenders before the fight begins. He enjoys being deceived.

It is altogether possible to practice fraud upon our own souls and go deceived to judgment. "If a man think himself to be something, when he is nothing," said Paul, "he deceiveth himself." With this agrees the inspired James: "If any man among you seem to be religious, and bridleth not his tongue, but deceiveth his own heart, this man's religion is vain."

The farther we push into the sanctuary the greater becomes the danger of self-deception. The deeply religious man is far more vulnerable than the easygoing fellow who takes his religion lightly. This latter may be deceived but he is not likely to be self-deceived.

Under the pressure of deep spiritual concern, and before his heart has been wholly conquered by the Spirit of God, a man may be driven to try every dodge to save face and preserve a semblance of his old independence. This is always dangerous and if persisted in may prove calamitous.

The fallen heart is by nature idolatrous. There appears to be no limit to which some of us will go to save our idol, while at the same time telling ourselves eagerly that we are trusting in Christ alone. It takes a violent act of renunciation to deliver us from the hidden idol, and since very few modern Christians understand that such an act is necessary, and only a small number of those who know are willing to do, it follows that relatively few professors of the Christian faith these days have ever experienced the painful act of renunciation that frees the heart from idolatry.

Prayer is usually recommended as the panacea for all ills and the key to open every prison door, and it would indeed be difficult to overstate the advantages and privilege of Spirit-inspired prayer. But we must not forget that unless we are wise and watchful prayer itself may become a source of self-deception. There are as many kinds of prayer as there are problems and some kinds are not acceptable to God. The prophets of the Old Testament denounced Israel for trying to hide their iniquities behind their prayers. Christ flatly rejected the prayers of hypocrites and James declared that some religious persons ask and receive not because they ask amiss.

To escape self-deception the praying man must come out clean and honest. He cannot hide in the cross while concealing in his bosom the golden wedge and the goodly Babylonish garment. Grace will save a man but it will not save him and his idol. The blood of Christ will shield the penitent sinner alone, but never the sinner and his idol. Faith will justify the sinner, but it will never justify the sinner and his sin.

No amount of pleading will make evil good or wrong right. A man may engage in a great deal of humble talk before God and get no response because unknown to himself he is using prayer to disguise disobedience. He may lie for hours in sackcloth and ashes with no higher motive than to try to persuade God to come over on his side so he can have his own way. He may grovel before God in a welter of self-accusation, refuse to give up his secret sin and be rejected for his pains. It can happen.

Dr. H. M. Shuman once said to me in private conversation that he believed the one quality God required a man to have before He would save him was honesty. With this I heartily agree. However dishonest the man may have been before, he must put away his duplicity if he is to be accepted before the Lord. Double dealing is unutterably offensive to God. The insincere man has no claim on mercy. For such a man the cross of Christ provides no remedy. Christ can and will save a man who has been dishonest, but He cannot save him while he is dishonest. Absolute candor is an indispensable requisite to salvation.

How may we remain free from self-deception? The answer sounds old-fashioned and dull but here it is: Mean what you say and never say what you do not mean, either to God or man. Think candid thoughts and act forthrightly always, whatever the consequence. To do this will bring the cross into your life and keep you dead to self and to public opinion. And it may get you into trouble sometimes, too. But a guileless mind is a great treasure; it is worth any price.

23
ON BREEDING SPOTTED MICE

The Associated Press lately carried an interesting if somewhat de-pressing story out of London about a certain British peer who had died just a few days short of his eighty-ninth birthday.

Having been a man of means and position, it had presumably not been necessary for him to work for a living like the rest of us, so at the time of his death he had had about seventy adult years in which he was free to do whatever he wanted to do, to pursue any calling he wished or to work at anything he felt worthy of his considerable abilities.

And what had he chosen to do? Well, according to the story, he had "devoted his life to trying to breed the perfect spotted mouse."

Now, I grant every man the right to breed spotted mice if he wants to and can get the cooperation of the mice, and I freely admit that it is his business and not mine. Not being a mouse lover (nor a mouse hater for that matter; I am just neutral about mice), I do not know but that a spotted mouse might be more useful and make a more affectionate pet than a common mouse colored mouse. But still I am troubled.

The mouse breeder in question was a lord, and I was born on a farm in the hill country of Pennsylvania, but since a cat can look at a king I suppose a farm boy can look at a lord, even look at him with disapproval if the circumstances warrant. Anyway, a man's a man for a' that, and I feel a certain kinship for every man born of woman; so I cannot but grieve for my brother beyond the seas.

Made in the image of God, equipped with awesome powers of mind and soul, called to dream immortal dreams and to think the long thoughts of eternity, he chooses the breeding of a spotted mouse as his reason for existing. Invited to walk with God on earth and to dwell at last with the saints and angels in the world above; called to serve his generation by the will of God, to press with holy vigor toward the mark for the prize of the high calling of God in Christ Jesus, he dedicates his life to the spotted mouse—not just evenings or holidays, mind you, but his entire life. Surely this is tragedy worthy of the mind of an Aeschylus or a Shakespeare.

Let us hope that the story is not true or that the news boys got it mixed up as they sometimes do; but even if the whole thing should prove to be a hoax, still it points up a stark human tragedy that is being enacted before our eyes daily, not by makebelieve play actors, but by real men and women who are the characters they portray. These should be concerned with sin and righteousness and judgment; they should be getting ready to die and to live again; but instead they spend their days breeding spotted mice.

If the spiritual view of the world is the correct one, as Christianity boldly asserts that it is, then for every one of us heaven is more important than earth and eternity more important than time. If Jesus Christ is who He claimed to be; if He is what the glorious company of the apostles and the noble army of martyrs declared that He is; if the faith which the holy church throughout all the world doth acknowledge is the true faith of God, then no man has any right to dedicate his life to anything that can burn or rust or rot or die. No man has any right to give himself completely to anyone but Christ nor to anything but prayer.

The man who does not know where he is is lost; the man who does not know why he was born is worse lost; the man who cannot find an object worthy of his true devotion is lost utterly; and by this description the human race is lost, and it is a part of our lostness that we do not know how lost we are. So we use up the few precious years allotted to us breeding spotted mice. Not the kind that scurry and squeak, maybe; but viewed in the light of eternity, are not most of our little human activities almost as meaningless?

One of the glories of the Christian gospel is its ability not only to deliver a man from sin but to orient him, to place him on a peak from which he can see yesterday and today in their relation to tomorrow. The truth cleanses his mind so that he can recognize things that matter and see time and space and kings and cabbages in their true perspective. The Spirit-illuminated Christian cannot be cheated. He knows the values of things; he will not bid on a rainbow nor make a down payment on a mirage; he will not, in short, devote his life to spotted mice.

Back of every wasted life is a bad philosophy, an erroneous conception of life's worth and purpose. The man who believes that he was born to get all be can will spend his life trying to get it; and whatever he gets will be but a cage of spotted mice. The man who believes he was created to enjoy fleshly pleasures will devote himself to pleasure seeking; and if by a combination of favorable circumstances he manages to get a lot of fun out of life, his pleasures will all turn to ashes in his mouth at the last. He will find out too late that God made him too noble to be satisfied with those tawdry pleasures he had devoted his life to here under the sun.

24
THE UNKNOWN SAINTS

William Wordsworth in a fine passage states his belief that there are many more poets in the world than we suppose,

> ". . .men endowed with highest gifts,
> The vision and the faculty divine,"

but who are unknown because they lacked or failed to cultivate the gift of versification.

Then he sums up his belief in a sentence that suggests truth far beyond any that he had in mind at the time:

> "Strongest minds
> Are often those of whom the noisy world
> Hears least."

Most of us in our soberer moments would admit the soundness of this observation, but the hard fact is that for the average person it is not the findings of the sober moment that determine our total working philosophy; rather it is the shallow and deceptive notions pressed upon us by the "noisy world." Human society generally (and especially in the United States) has fallen into the error of assuming that greatness and fame are synonymous. Americans appear to take for granted that each generation provides a certain number of superior men and the democratic processes unerringly find those men and set them in a place of prominence. How wrong can people get!

We have but to become acquainted with, or even listen to, the big names of our times to discover how wretchedly inferior most of them are. Many appear to have arrived at their present eminence by pull, brass, nerve, gall and lucky accident. We turn away from them sick to our stomach and wonder for a discouraged moment if this is the best the human race can produce. But we gain our self-possession again by the simple expedient of recalling some of the plain men we know, who live unheralded and unsung, and who are made of stuff infinitely finer than the hoarse-voiced braggarts who occupy too many of the highest offices in the land.

If we would see life steadily and see it whole we must make a stern effort to break away from the power of that false philosophy that equates greatness with fame. The two may be and often are oceans and continents apart.

If the church were a body wholly unaffected by the world we could toss the above problem over to the secular philosophers and go about our business; but the truth is that the church also suffers from this evil notion. Christians have fallen into the habit of accepting the noisiest and most notorious among them as the best and the greatest. They too have learned to equate popularity with excellence, and in open defiance of the Sermon on the Mount they have given their approval not to the meek but to the self-assertive; not to the mourner but to the self-assured; not to the pure in heart who see God but to the publicity hunter who seeks headlines.

If we might paraphrase Wordsworth we could make his lines run,

> "Purest saints
> Are often those of whom the noisy church
> Hears least,"

and the words would be true, deeply, wonderfully true.

After more than thirty years of observing the religious scene I have been forced to conclude that saintliness and church leadership are not often synonymous. I have on many occasions preached to grateful Christians who had gone so much farther than I had into the sweet mysteries of God that I actually felt unworthy to tie their shoe laces. Yet they sat meekly listening while one inferior to them stood in the place of prominence and declared imperfectly truths with which they had long been familiar by intimate and beautiful experience. They must have known and felt how much of theory and how little of real heart knowledge there was in the sermon, but they said nothing and no doubt appreciated what little of good there was in the message.

Were the church a pure and Spirit-filled body, wholly led and directed by spiritual considerations, certainly the purest and the saintliest men and women would be the ones most appreciated and most honored; but the opposite is true. Godliness is no longer valued, except for the very old or the very dead. The saintly souls are forgotten in the whirl of religious activity. The noisy, the self-assertive, the entertaining are sought after and rewarded in every way, with gifts, crowds, offerings and publicity. The Christ-like, the self-forgetting, the other-worldly are jostled aside to make room for the latest converted playboy who is usually not too well converted and still very much of a playboy.

The whole short-sighted philosophy that ignores eternal qualities and majors on trivialities is a form of unbelief. These Christians who embody such a philosophy are clamoring after present reward; they are too impatient to wait the Lord's time. They will not abide the day when Christ shall make known the secret of every man's heart and reward each one according to his deeds. The true saint sees farther than this; he cares little for passing values; he looks forward eagerly to the day when eternal things shall come into their own and godliness will be found to be all that matters.

Strange as it may be, the holiest souls who have ever lived have earned the reputation for being pessimistic. Their smiling indifference to the world's attractions and their steady resistance to its temptations have been misunderstood by shallow thinkers and attributed to an unsocial spirit and a lack of love for mankind. What the world failed to see was that these peculiar men and women were beholding a city invisible; they were walking day by day in the light of another and eternal kingdom. They were already tasting the powers of the world to come and enjoying afar the triumph of Christ and the glories of the new creation.

No, the unknown saints are riot pessimists, nor are they misanthropes or joy-killers. They are by virtue of their godly faith the world's only true optimists. Their creed was stated simply by Julian of Norwich when she said, "But all shall be well, and all shall be well, and all manner of thing shall be well." Though sin is in the world, she argued, a frightful visitation to be reckoned with, yet so perfect is the atonement that the time will come when all evil shall be eradicated and everything restored again to its pristine beauty in Christ. Then "all shall be well, and all manner of thing shall be well."

The wise Christian will be content to wait for that day. In the meantime, he will serve his generation in the will of God. If he should be overlooked in the religious popularity contests he will give it but small attention. He knows whom he is trying to please and he is willing to let the world think what it will of him. He will not be around much longer anyway, and where he is going men will be known not by their 'Hooper' rating but by the holiness of their character.

25
THREE FAITHFUL WOUNDS

Faithful are the wounds of a friend, says the Holy Spirit in Proverbs 27:6. And lest we imagine that the preacher is the one who does the wounding, I want to read Job 5:17 and 18: "Behold, happy is the man whom God correcteth: therefore despise not thou the chastening of the Almighty: for he maketh sore, and bindeth up: he woundeth, and his hands make whole." You see, the one who does the wounding here is not the servant, but the Master Himself. So with that in our minds I want to talk to you about three faithful wounds of a friend.

In order to get launched into my message let me introduce a little lady who has been dead for about six hundred years. She once lived and loved and prayed and sang in the city of Norwich, England. This little woman hadn't much light and she hadn't any way to get much light, but the beautiful thing about her was that, with what little Biblical light she had, she walked with God so wonderfully close that she became as fragrant as a flower. And long before Reformation times she was in spirit an evangelical. She lived and died and has now been with her Lord nearly six hundred years, but she has left behind her a fragrance of Christ.

England was a better place because this little lady lived. She wrote only one book, a very tiny book that you could slip into your side pocket or your purse, but it's so flavorful, so divine, so heavenly, that it has made a distinct contribution to the great spiritual literature of the world. The lady to whom I refer is the one called the Lady Julian.

Before she blossomed out into this radiant, glorious life which made her famous as a great Christian all over her part of the world, she prayed a prayer and God answered. It is this prayer with which I am concerned tonight. The essence of her prayer was this:

"O God, please give me three wounds; the wound of contrition and the wound of compassion and the wound of longing after God." Then she added this little postscript which I think is one of the most beautiful things I have ever read: "This I ask without condition." She wasn't dickering with God. She wanted three things and they were all for God's glory: "I ask this without condition, Father; do what I ask and then send me the bill. Anything that it costs will be all right with me."

All great Christians have been wounded souls. It is strange what a wound will do to a man. Here's a soldier who goes out to the battlefield. He is full of jokes and strength and self-assurance; then one day a piece of shrapnel tears through him and he falls, a whimpering, beaten, defeated man. Suddenly his whole world collapses around him and this man, instead of being the great, strong, broad-chested fellow that he thought he was, suddenly becomes a whimpering boy again. And such have ever been known, I am told, to cry for their mothers when they lie bleeding and suffering on the field of battle. There is nothing like a wound to take the self-assurance out of us, to reduce us to childhood again and make us small and helpless in our own sight.

Many of the Old Testament characters were wounded men, stricken of God and afflicted indeed as their Lord was after them. Take Jacob, for instance. Twice God afflicted him; twice he met God and each time it came as a wound, and one time it came actually as a physical wound and he limped on his thigh for the rest of his life. And the man Elijah-was he not more than a theologian, more than a doctrinarian? He was a man who had been stricken; he had been struck with the sword of God and was no longer simply one of Adam's race standing up in his own self-assurance; he was a man who had had an encounter with God, who had been confronted by God and had been defeated and broken down before Him. And when Isaiah saw the Lord high and lifted up, you know what it did to him. Or take the man Ezekiel, how he went down before his God and became a little child again. And there were many others.

Now the wounded man is a defeated man, I say; the strong, robust and self-confident Adam-man ceases to fight back any longer; he lays down his sword and surrenders and the wound finishes him. Let's talk about these three wounds in their order.

The first is the wound of contrition. Now I've heard for the last thirty years that repentance is a change of mind, and I believe it, of course, as far as it goes. But that's just what's the matter with us. We have reduced repentance to a change of mind. It is a mental act, indeed, but I point out that repentance is not likely to do us much good until it ceases to be a change of mind only and becomes a wound within our spirit. No man has truly repented until his sin has wounded him near to death, until the wound has broken him and defeated him and taken all the fight and self-assurance out of him and he sees himself as the one who nailed his Saviour on the tree.

I don't know about you, but the only way I can keep right with God is to keep contrite, to keep a sense of contrition upon my spirit. Now there's a lot of cheap and easy getting rid of sin and getting your repentance disposed of. But the great Christians, in and out of the Bible, have been those who were wounded with a sense of contrition so that they never quite got over the thought and the feeling that they personally had crucified Jesus. The great Bishop Usher each week used to go down by the riverbank and there all Saturday afternoon kneel by a log and bewail his sins before his God. Perhaps that was the secret of his greatness.

Let us beware of vain and over-hasty repentance, and particularly let us beware of no repentance at all. We are a sinful race, ladies and gentlemen, a sinful people, and until the knowledge has hit hard, until it has wounded us, until it has got through and past the little department of our theology, it has done us no good. A man can believe in total depravity and never have any sense of it for himself at all. Lots of us believe in total depravity who have never been wounded with the knowledge that we've sinned. Repentance is a wound I pray we may all feel.

And then there's the wound of compassion. Now compassion is an emotional identification, and Christ had that in full perfection. The man who has this wound of compassion is a man who suffers along with other people. Jesus Christ our Lord can never suffer to save us any more. This He did, once for all, when He gave Himself without spot through the Holy Ghost to the Father on Calvary's cross. He cannot suffer to save us but He still must suffer to win us. He does not call His people to redemptive suffering. That's impossible; it could not be. Redemption is a finished work.

But He does call His people to feel along with Him and to feel along with those that rejoice and those that suffer. He calls His people to be to Him the kind of an earthly body in which He can weep again and suffer again and love again. For our Lord has two bodies. One is the body He took to the tree on Calvary; that was the body in which He suffered to redeem us. But He has a body on earth now, composed of those who have been baptized into it by the Holy Ghost at conversion. In that body He would now suffer to win men. Paul said that he was glad that he could suffer for the Colossians and fill up the measure of the afflictions of Christ in his body for the church's sake.

Now, my brethren, I don't know whether I can make it clear or not. I know that things like this have to be felt rather than understood, but the wounded man is never a seeker after happiness. There is an ignoble pursuit of irresponsible happiness among us. Over the last years, as I have observed the human scene and have watched God's professed people live and die, I have seen that most of us would rather be happy than to feel the wounds of other people's sorrows. I do not believe that it is the will of God that we should seek to be happy, but rather that we should seek to be holy and useful. The holy man will be the useful man and he's likely to be a happy man too; but if he seeks happiness and forgets holiness and usefulness, he's a carnal man. I, for one, want no part in carnal religious joy. There are times when it's sinful to be happy. When Jesus our Lord was sweating it out there in the garden or hanging on the tree, He could not be happy. He was the "man of sorrows, and acquainted with grief."

And the great saints of the past, who conquered and captured parts of the world for Jesus, when they were in travail were not happy. The woman, said Jesus, who is giving birth is not happy at the time of her travail, but as soon as the child is delivered she becomes happy because a man is born into the world. You and I are, in a sense, to be mothers in Israel, those through whom the Lord can suffer and grieve and love and pity again to bring children to birth.

Thirdly, there's the wound of longing after God. This little woman wanted to long after God with a longing that became a pain in her heart. She wanted to be lovesick. She prayed in effect, "O God, that I might want Thee so badly that it becomes a wound in my heart that I can't get over." Today, accepting Christ becomes terminal. That is the end. And all evangelism leads toward one thing-getting increased numbers of people to accept Christ, and there we put a period. My criticism of most of our Bible conferences is that we spend our time counting again the treasures that we have in Christ but we never arrive at the place where any of that which is in Christ gets into us. He has blessed us with all spiritual blessings in the heavenly places in Christ, but you can no more buy food with the money still in the bank than you can live on the treasures that are in Christ unless they're also experientially in you.

So many of us say, "All right, I'll attend another Bible conference," or "I'll take a course," or "I'll buy a book." My friends, what we need is not more instruction; we've been instructed to death. Where in the world is there more fundamental Bible teaching than here in Chicago? This is the Mecca of Fundamentalism. This is the Vatican of Evangelicalism. We've got notebooks at home stacked high that go back twenty-five years. They tell us of some new sidelight on some text or some new illustration somebody gave to point up a doctrine. But, oh, what weak creatures we are! What joyless people we are!

Note the paradoxes: To be happily forgiven and yet to be wounded and to remember the grief; to enjoy the peace of the finished work of Christ and yet suffer to win others; to find God and yet be always pursuing Him. When Moses saw the glory of God he begged that he might see more. When God revealed to him that he had found grace, he wanted more grace. Remember this: the man that has the most of God is the man who is seeking the most ardently for more of God.

There was a man who talked about "a restless thirst, a sacred, infinite desire," and that is what I want for my own heart. Among the plastic saints of our times Jesus has to do all the dying and all we want is to hear another sermon about His dying; Jesus does all the sorrowing and we want to be happy. But, my brethren, if we were what we ought to be, we would seek to know in experience the meaning of the words, "Except a corn of wheat fall into the ground and die, it abideth alone: but if it die, it bringeth forth much fruit."

I have been greatly and deeply concerned that you and I do something more than listen, that we dare to go to God like the Lady Julian and dare to ask Him to give us a faithful, fatherly wound-maybe three of them, if you please: to wound us with a sense of our own sinful unworthiness that we'll never quite get over; to wound us with the sufferings of the world and the sorrows of the church; and then to wound us with the longing after God, a thirst, a sacred thirst and longing that will carry us on toward perfection.

> The lack of desire is the ill of all ills;
> Many thousands through it the dark pathway have trod;
> The balsam, the wine of predestinate wills,

Is a jubilant pining and longing for God.
—Frederick W. Faber

Write that sentence down, "A jubilant pining and longing for God." Almost every day of my life I am praying that "a jubilant pining and longing for God" might come back on the evangelical churches. We don't need to have our doctrine straightened out; we're as orthodox as the Pharisees of old. But this longing for God that brings spiritual torrents and whirlwinds of seeking and self-denial-this is almost gone from our midst.

God loves to be longed for, He loves to be sought,
For He sought us Himself with such longing and love;
He died for desire of us, marvelous thought!
And He longs for us now to be with Him above.
—Frederick W. Faber

I believe that God wants us to long for Him with the longing that will become lovesickness, that will become a wound to our spirits, to keep us always moving toward Him, always finding and always seeking, always having and always desiring. So the earth becomes less and less valuable and heaven gets closer as we move into God and up into Christ.

Dare we bow our hearts now and say, "Father, I've been an irresponsible, childish kind of Christian-more concerned with being happy than with being holy. O God, give me three wounds. Wound me with a sense of my own sinfulness. Wound me with compassion for the world, and wound me with love of Thee that will keep me always pursuing and always exploring and always seeking and always finding."

If you dare to pray that prayer sincerely and mean it before God, it could mean a turning point in your life. It could mean a door of victory opened to you. May God grant that it be so.

26
THE WRATH OF GOD: WHAT IS IT?

It is rare that there is anything good in human anger. Almost always it springs out of unholy states of heart, and frequently it leads to cursing and violence. The man of evil temper is unpredictable and dangerous and is usually shunned by men of peace and good will.

There is a strong tendency among religious teachers these days to disassociate anger from the divine character and to defend God by explaining away the Scriptures that relate it to Him. This is understandable, but in the light of the full revelation of God it is inexcusable.

In the first place, God needs no defense. Those teachers who are forever trying to make God over in their own image might better be employed in seeking to make themselves over in the image of God. In the Scriptures "God spake all these words," and there is no independent criterion by which we can judge the revelation God there makes concerning Himself.

The present refusal of so many to accept the doctrine of the wrath of God is part of a larger pattern of unbelief that begins with doubt concerning the veracity of the Christian Scriptures.

Let a man question the inspiration of the Scriptures and a curious, even monstrous, inversion takes place: thereafter he judges the Word instead of letting the Word judge him; he determines what the Word should teach instead of permitting it to determine what he should believe; he edits, amends, strikes out, adds at his pleasure; but always he sits above the Word and makes it amenable to him instead of kneeling before God and becoming amenable to the Word.

The tender-minded interpreter who seeks to shield God from the implications of His own Word is engaged in an officious effort that cannot but be completely wasted.

Why such a man still clings to the tattered relics of religion it is hard to say. The manly thing would be to walk out on the Christian faith and put it behind him along with other outgrown toys and discredited beliefs of childhood, but this he rarely does. He kills the tree but still hovers pensively about the orchard hoping for fruit that never comes.

Whatever is stated clearly but once in the Holy Scriptures may be accepted as sufficiently well established to invite the faith of all believers; and when we discover that the Spirit speaks of the wrath of God about three hundred times in the Bible we may as well make up our minds either to accept the doctrine or reject the Scriptures outright. If we have valid information from some outside source proving that anger is unworthy of God, then the Bible is not to be trusted when it attributes anger to God. And if it is wrong three hundred times on one subject, who can trust it on any other?

The instructed Christian knows that the wrath of God is a reality, that His anger is as holy as His love, and that between His love and His wrath there is no incompatibility. He further knows (as far as fallen creatures can know such matters) what the wrath of God is and what it is not.

To understand God's wrath we must view it in the light of His holiness. God is holy and has made holiness to be the moral condition necessary to the health of His universe. Sin's temporary presence in the world only accents this. Whatever is holy is healthy; evil is a moral sickness that must end ultimately in death. The formation of the language itself suggests this, the English word holy deriving from the Anglo-Saxon halig, hal meaning well, whole. While it is not wise to press word origins unduly, there is yet a significance here that should not be overlooked.

Since God's first concern for His universe is its moral health, that is, its holiness, whatever is contrary to this is necessarily under His eternal displeasure. Wherever the holiness of God confronts unholiness there is conflict. This conflict arises from the irreconcilable natures of holiness and sin. God's attitude and action in the conflict are His anger. To preserve His creation God must destroy whatever would destroy it. When He arises to put down destruction and save the world from irreparable moral collapse He is said to be angry. Every wrathful judgment of God in the history of the world has been a holy act of preservation.

The holiness of God, the wrath of God and the health of the creation are inseparably united. Not only is it right for God to display anger against sin, but I find it impossible to understand how He could do otherwise.

God's wrath is His utter intolerance of whatever degrades and destroys. He hates iniquity as a mother hates the diphtheria or polio that would destroy the life of her child.

God's wrath is the antisepsis by which moral putrefaction is checked and the health of the creation maintained. When God warns of His impending wrath and exhorts men to repent and avoid it He puts it in a language they can understand: He tells them to "flee from the wrath to come." He says in effect, "Your life is evil, and because it is evil you are an enemy to the moral health of My creation. I must extirpate whatever would destroy the world I love. Turn from evil before I rise up in wrath against you. I love you, but I hate the sin you love. Separate yourself from your evil ways before I send judgment upon you."

"O Lord,- . . in wrath remember mercy" (Hab. 3:2).

27
IN PRAISE OF DOGMATISM

It is vital to any understanding of ourselves and our fellowmen that we believe what is written in the Scriptures about human society, that it is fallen, alienated from God and in rebellion against His laws.

In these days of togetherness when all men would brothers be for a' that, even the true Christian is hard put to it to believe what God has spoken about men and their relation to each other and to God; for what He has spoken is never complimentary to men.

There is plenty of good news in the Bible, but there is never any flattery or back scratching. Seen one way, the Bible is a book of doom. It condemns all men as sinners and declares that the soul that sinneth shall die. Always it pronounces sentence against society before it offers mercy; and if we will not own the validity of the sentence we cannot admit the need for mercy.

The coming of Jesus Christ to the world has been so sentimentalized that it means now something utterly alien to the Biblical teaching concerning it. Soft human pity has been substituted for God's mercy in the minds of millions, a pity that has long ago degenerated into self-pity. The blame for man's condition has been shifted to God, and Christ's dying for the world has been twisted into an act of penance on God's part. In the drama of redemption man is viewed as Miss Cinderella who has long been oppressed and mistreated, but now through the heroic deeds of earth's noblest Son is about to don her radiant apparel and step forth a queen.

This is humanism romantically tinted with Christianity, a humanism that takes sides with rebels and excuses those who by word, thought and deed would glorify fallen men and if possible overthrow the glorious high Throne in the heavens.

According to this philosophy men are never really to blame for anything, the exception being the man who insists that men are indeed to blame for something. In this dim world of pious sentiment all religions are equal and any man who insists that salvation is by Jesus Christ alone is a bigot and a boor.

So we pool our religious light, which if the truth is told is little more than darkness visible; we discuss religion on television and in the press as a kind of game, much as we discuss art and philosophy, accepting as one of the ground rules of the game that there is no final test of truth and that the best religion is a composite of the best in all religions. So we have truth by majority vote and thus saith the Lord by common consent.

One characteristic of this sort of thing is its timidity. That religion may be very precious to some persons is admitted, but never important enough to cause division or risk hurting anyone's feelings. In all our discussions there must never be any trace of intolerance; but we obviously forget that the most fervent devotees of tolerance are invariably intolerant of everyone who speaks about God with certainty. And there must be no bigotry, which is the name given to spiritual assurance by those who do not enjoy it.

The desire to please may be commendable enough under certain circumstances, but when pleasing men means displeasing God it is an unqualified evil and should have no place in the Christian's heart. To be right with God has often meant to be in trouble with men. This is such a common truth that one hesitates to mention it, yet it appears to have been overlooked by the majority of Christians today.

There is a notion abroad that to win a man we must agree with him. Actually the exact opposite is true. G. K. Chesterton remarked that each generation has had to be converted by the man who contradicted it most. The man who is going in a wrong direction will never be set right by the affable religionist who falls into step beside him and goes the same way. Someone must place himself across the path and insist that the straying man turn around and go in the right direction.

There is of course a sense in which we are all in this terrible human mess together, and for this reason there are certain areas of normal activity where we can all agree. The Christian will not disagree merely to be different, but wherever the moral standards and religious views of society differ from the teachings of Christ he will disagree flatly. He will not admit the validity of human opinion when the Word of God is clear. Some things are not debatable; there is no other side to them. There is only God's side.

When men believe God they speak boldly. When they doubt they confer. Much current religious talk is but uncertainty rationalizing itself; and this they call "engaging in the contemporary dialogue." It is impossible to imagine Moses or Elijah so occupied.

All great Christian leaders have been dogmatic. To such men two plus two made four. Anyone who insisted upon denying it or suspending judgment upon it was summarily dismissed as frivolous. They were only interested in a meeting of minds if the minds agreed to meet on holy ground. We could use some gentle dogmatists these days.

28
WHAT MEN LIVE BY

Human life has its central core where lie the things men live by. These things are constant. They change not from age to age, but are the same among all races throughout the world always.

Life also has its marginal zones where lie the things that are relatively unimportant. These change from generation to generation and vary from people to people.

It is at the central core that men are one, and it is on the marginal zones that they differ from each other. Yet the marginal things divide the peoples of the world radically and seriously. Most of the enmities of the earth have arisen from differences that did not matter basically; but because the people could not distinguish things men live by from things they live with these enmities arose between them, and often led to persecutions, murders and bloody wars.

Were men everywhere to ignore the things that matter little or not at all and give serious attention to the few really important things, most of the walls that divide men would be thrown down at once and a world of endless sufferings ended.

What does matter after all? What are the great facts that are good all the time everywhere among all men? What are the axiomatic truths upon which all human life may rest with confidence? Fortunately they are not many. Here are the chief ones:

1. Only God is great. Men have sought to place greatness elsewhere, in things, in events, in men; but the human soul is too great to attribute greatness to itself, and certainly too great to believe that things or events can possess true greatness.

The greatness that men seem to have is as the greatness of moonlight, which is but the glory of the sun reflected. Man's glory is borrowed. He shines in the light that never was on land or sea. He reflects God's greatness but has none of his own.

"Before Thy ever-blazing throne We ask no luster of our own."*

2. Only God is wise. Man's wisdom has ever been the badge of his superiority and the cause of his most arrogant pride; yet it fails him constantly. He cannot by his wisdom find the answer to the old questions concerning himself: Whence? What? Why? Whither? By it he cannot secure the blessings he wants most: to escape pain, to stay young and to stay alive.

Yet man boasts of his wisdom, God waits, the ages pass, and time and space and matter and motion and life and death join to tell us that only God is wise.

3. Apart from God nothing matters. We think that health matters, that freedom matters, or knowledge or art or civilization. And but for one insistent word they would matter indeed. That word is eternity.

Grant that men possess perpetual being and the preciousness of every earthly treasure is gone instantly. God is to our eternal being what our heart is to our body. The lungs, the liver, the kidneys have value as they relate to the heart. Let the heart stop and the rest of the organs promptly collapse. Apart from God, what is money, fame, education, civilization? Exactly nothing at all, for men must leave all these things behind them and one by one go to eternity. Let God hide His face and nothing thereafter is worth the effort.

4. Only what we do in God will remain to us at last.

Man is made in the image of his Creator and has an urge toward creative activity. When he left the Garden his creative urge did not leave him. He must build, always build; his materials may be brick, paint, musical notes, scientific data, systems of thought; but always he must build, from the boy that builds a toy to the man that builds an empire.

Yet time is against him, for it wears out everything it touches. Its grinding action makes dust of civilizations and cities and men. A lifetime of toil dies with the toiler. But God puts immortality in all our loving efforts for Him and shares His eternity with all who love and trust Him.

5. Human sin is real. Suspicion, hate, envy, power, lust and greed keep the world in a state of continual ferment, while bespectacled men stand unblinking and assure classes of eager students that the whole idea

of sin is outmoded and sin itself non-existent.

In spite of all our smooth talk sin continues to ride the race of man. Until its heavy weight is lifted from the soul nothing else has any right to our attention, for sin shuts us out from the presence of the God whose favor alone gives life any satisfactory reason for being.

6. With God there is forgiveness. "The Lord God, merciful and gracious . . . keeping mercy for thousands, forgiving iniquity and transgression and sin." So says the Old Testament. (Ex. 34:6) "The Son of man hath power on earth to forgive sins," says the New. (Matt. 9:6)

God's mercy heads up in the Man Christ Jesus who is God and man by the mystery of the Incarnation. He can and does forgive sin because the sin was committed against Him in the first place. The soul in Christ has found the One that matters. His heaviest problem is solved; his basic philosophy is sound; his eyes are open and he knows the true from the false.

7. Only what God protects is safe. All else perishes with the using or the hoarding. Paul knew this secret. He said, "He is able to keep that which I have committed unto him against that day." (2 Tim. 1:12)

Blessed Treasure. Blessed Keeper. Blessed Day.

29
HOW TO TRY THE SPIRITS

These are the times that try men's souls. The Spirit has spoken expressly that in the latter times some should depart from the faith, giving heed to seducing spirits and doctrines of demons; speaking lies in hypocrisy; having their conscience seared with a hot iron. Those days are upon us and we cannot escape them; we must triumph in the midst of them, for such is the will of God concerning us.

Strange as it may seem, the danger today is greater for the fervent Christian than for the lukewarm and the self-satisfied. The seeker after God's best things is eager to hear anyone who offers a way by which he can obtain them. He longs for some new experience, some elevated view of truth, some operation of the Spirit that will raise him above the dead level of religious mediocrity he sees all around him, and for this reason he is ready to give a sympathetic ear to the new and the wonderful in religion, particularly if it is presented by someone with an attractive personality and a reputation for superior godliness.

Now our Lord Jesus. that great Shepherd of the sheep, has not left His flock to the mercy of the wolves. He has given us the Scriptures, the Holy Spirit and natural powers of observation, and He expects us to avail ourselves of their help constantly. "Prove all things; hold fast that which is good," said Paul (I Thess. 5:21) . "Beloved, believe not every spirit," wrote John, "but try the spirits whether they are of God: because many false prophets are gone out into the world" (I John 4:1) . "Beware of false prophets," our Lord warned, "which come to you in sheep's clothing, but inwardly they are ravening wolves" (Matt. 7:15). Then He added the word by which they may be tested, "Ye shall know them by their fruits."

From this it is plain not only that there shall be false spirits abroad, endangering our Christian lives, but that they may be identified and known for what they are. And of course once we become aware of their identity and learn their tricks their power to harm us is gone. "Surely in vain the net is spread in the sight of any bird" (Prov. 1:17)

It is my intention to set forth here a method by which we may test the spirits and prove all things religious and moral that come to us or are brought or offered to us by anyone. And while dealing with these matters we should keep in mind that not all religious vagaries are the work of Satan. The human mind is capable of plenty of mischief without any help from the devil. Some persons have a positive genius for getting confused, and will mistake illusion for reality in broad daylight with the Bible open before them. Peter had such in mind when he wrote, "Our beloved brother Paul also according to the wisdom given unto him hath written unto you; as also in all his epistles, speaking in them of these things; in which are some things hard to be understood, which they that are unlearned and unstable wrest, as they do also the other scriptures, unto their own destruction" (II Pet. 3:15, 16).

It is unlikely that the confirmed apostles of confusion will read what is written here or that they would profit much if they did; but there are many sensible Christians who have been led astray but are humble enough to admit their mistakes and are now ready to return unto the Shepherd and Bishop of their souls. These may be rescued from false paths. More important still, there are undoubtedly large numbers of persons who have not left the true way but who want a rule by which they can test everything and by which they may prove the quality of Christian teaching and experience as they come in contact with them day after day throughout their busy lives. For such as these I make available here a little secret by which I have tested my own spiritual experiences and religious impulses for many years.

Briefly stated the test is this: This new doctrine, this new religious habit, this new view of truth, this new spiritual experience how has it affected my attitude toward and my relation to God, Christ, the Holy Scriptures, self, other Christians, the world and sin. By this sevenfold test we may prove everything religious and know beyond a doubt whether it is of God or not. By the fruit of the tree we know the kind of tree it is. So we have but to ask about any doctrine or experience, What is this doing to me? and we know immediately whether it is from above or from below.

1) One vital test of all religious experience is how it affects our relation to God, our concept of God and our attitude toward Him. God being who He is must always be the supreme arbiter of all things religious. The universe came into existence as a medium through which the Creator might show forth His perfections to all moral and intellectual beings: "I am the Lord: that is my name: and my glory will I not give to another" (Isa. 42: 8) . "Thou art worthy, O Lord, to receive glory and honour and power: for thou hast created all things, and for thy pleasure they are and were created" (Rev. 4:11).

The health and balance of the universe require that in all things God should be magnified. "Great is the Lord, and greatly to be praised; and his greatness is unsearchable." God acts only for His glory and whatever comes from Him must be to His own high honor. Any doctrine, any experience that serves to magnify Him is likely to be inspired by Him. Conversely, anything that veils His glory or makes Him appear less wonderful is sure to be of the flesh or the devil.

The heart of man is like a musical instrument and may be played upon by the Holy Spirit, by an evil spirit or by the spirit of man himself. Religious emotions are very much the same, no matter who the player may be. Many enjoyable feelings may be aroused within the soul by low or even idolatrous worship. The nun who kneels "breathless with adoration" before an image of the Virgin is having a genuine religious experience. She feels love, awe and reverence, all enjoyable emotions, as certainly as if she were adoring God. The mystical experiences of Hindus and Sufis cannot be brushed aside as mere pretense. Neither dare we dismiss the high religious flights of spiritists and other occultists as imagination. These may have and sometimes do have genuine encounters with something or someone beyond themselves. In the same manner Christians are sometimes led into emotional experiences that are beyond their power to comprehend. I have met such and they have inquired eagerly whether or not their experience was of God.

The big test is, What has this done to my relationship to the God and Father of our Lord Jesus Christ? If this new view of truth-this new encounter with spiritual things-has made me love God more, if it has magnified Him in my eyes, if it has purified my concept of His being and caused Him to appear more wonderful than before, then I may conclude that I have not wandered astray into the pleasant but dangerous and forbidden paths of error.

2. The next test is: How has this new experience affected my attitude toward the Lord Jesus Christ? Whatever place present-day religion may give to Christ, God gives Him top place in earth and in heaven. "This is my beloved Son, in whom I am well pleased," spoke the voice of God from heaven concerning our Lord Jesus. Peter, full of the Holy Spirit, declared: "God hath made that same Jesus, whom ye have crucified, both Lord and Christ" (Acts 2:36). Jesus said of Himself, "I am the way, the truth, and the life: no man cometh unto the Father, but by me." Again Peter said of Him, "Neither is there salvation in any other: for there is none other name under heaven given among men, whereby we must be saved" (Acts 4:12) . The whole book of Hebrews is devoted to the idea that Christ is above all others. He is shown to be above Aaron and Moses, and even the angels are called to fall down and worship Him. Paul says that He is the image of the invisible God, that in Him dwells the fullness of the Godhead bodily and that in all things He must have the preeminence. But time would fail me to tell of the glory accorded Him by prophets, patriarchs, apostles, saints, elders, psalmists, kings and seraphim. He is made unto us wisdom and righteousness and sanctification and redemption. He is our hope, our life, our all and all, now and forevermore.

All this being true, it is clear that He must stand at the center of all true doctrine, all acceptable practice and all genuine Christian experience. Anything that makes Him less than God has declared Him to be is delusion pure and simple and must be rejected, no matter how delightful or how satisfying it may for the time seem to be.

Christless Christianity sounds contradictory but it exists as a real phenomenon in our day. Much that is being done in Christ's name is false to Christ in that it is conceived by the flesh, incorporates fleshly methods, and seeks fleshly ends. Christ is mentioned from time to time in the same way and for the same reason that a self-seeking politician mentions Lincoln and the flag, to provide a sacred front for carnal activities and to deceive the simplehearted listeners. This giveaway is that Christ is not central: He is not all and in all.

Again, there are psychic experiences that thrill the seeker and lead him to believe that he has indeed met the Lord and been carried to the third heaven; but the true nature of the phenomenon is discovered later when the face of Christ begins to fade from the victim's consciousness and he comes to depend more and more upon emotional jags as a proof of his spirituality.

If on the other hand the new experience tends to make Christ indispensable, if it takes our interest off our feeling and places it in Christ, we are on the right track. Whatever makes Christ dear to us is pretty sure to be from God.

3. Another revealing test of the soundness of religious experience is, How does it affect my attitude toward the Holy Scriptures? Did this new experience, this new view of truth, spring out of the Word of God itself or was it the result of some stimulus that lay outside the Bible? Tender-hearted Christians often become victims of strong psychological pressure applied intentionally or innocently by someone's personal testimony, or by a colorful story told by a fervent preacher who may speak with prophetic finality but who has not checked his story with the facts nor tested the soundness of his conclusions by the Word of God.

Whatever originates outside the Scriptures should for that very reason be suspect until it can be shown to be in accord with them. If it should be found to be contrary to the Word of revealed truth no true Christian will accept it as being from God. However high the emotional content, no experience can be proved to be genuine unless we can find chapter and verse authority for it in the Scriptures. "To the word and to the testimony" must always be the last and final proof.

Whatever is new or singular should also be viewed with a lot of caution until it can furnish scriptural proof of its validity. Over the last half-century quite a number of unscriptural notions have gained acceptance among Christians by claiming that they were among the truths that were to be revealed in the last days. To be sure, say the advocates of this latter-daylight theory, Augustine did not know, Luther did not, John Knox, Wesley, Finney and Spurgeon did not understand this; but greater light has now shined upon God's people and we of these last days have the advantage of fuller revelation. We should not question the new doctrine nor draw back from this advanced experience. The Lord is getting His Bride ready for the marriage supper of the Lamb. We should all yield to this new movement of the Spirit. So they tell us.

The truth is that the Bible does not teach that there will be new light and advanced spiritual experiences in the latter days; it teaches the exact opposite. Nothing in Daniel or the New Testament epistles can be tortured into advocating the idea that we of the end of the Christian era shall enjoy light that was not known at its beginning. Beware of any man who claims to be wiser than the apostles or holier than the martyrs of the Early Church. The best way to deal with him is to rise and leave his presence. You cannot help him and he surely cannot help you.

Granted, however, that the Scriptures may not always be clear and that there are differences of interpretation among equally sincere men, this test will furnish all the proof needed of anything religious, viz., What does it do to my love for and appreciation of the Scriptures?

While true power lies not in the letter of the text but in the Spirit that inspired it, we should never underestimate the value of the letter. The text of truth has the same relation to truth as the honeycomb has to honey. One serves as a receptacle for the other. But there the analogy ends. The honey can be removed from the comb, but the Spirit of truth cannot and does not operate apart from the letter of the Holy Scriptures.

For this reason a growing acquaintance with the Holy Spirit will always mean an increasing love for the Bible. The Scriptures are in print what Christ is in person. The inspired Word is like a faithful portrait of Christ. But again the figure breaks down. Christ is in the Bible as no one can be in a mere portrait, for the Bible is a book of holy ideas and the eternal Word of the Father can and does dwell in the thought He has Himself inspired. Thoughts are things, and the thoughts of the Holy Scriptures form a lofty temple for the dwelling place of God.

From this it follows naturally that a true lover of God will be also a lover of His Word. Anything that comes to us from the God of the Word will deepen our love for the Word of God. This follows logically, but we have confirmation by a witness vastly more trustworthy than logic, viz., the concerted testimony of a great army of witnesses living and dead. These declare with one voice that their love for the Scriptures intensified as their faith mounted and their obedience became consistent and joyous.

If the new doctrine, the influence of that new teacher, the new emotional experience fills my heart with an avid hunger to meditate in the Scriptures day and night. I have every reason to believe that God has spoken to my soul and that my experience is genuine. Conversely, if my love for the Scriptures has cooled even a little, if my eagerness to eat and drink of the inspired Word has abated by as much as one degree, I should humbly admit that I have missed God's signal somewhere and frankly backtrack until I find the true way once more.

4. Again, we can prove the quality of religious experience by its effect on the self-life.

The Holy Spirit and the fallen human self are diametrically opposed to each other. "The flesh lusteth against the Spirit, and the Spirit against the flesh: and these are contrary the one to the other: so that ye cannot do the things that ye would" (Gal. 5:17). "They that are after the flesh do mind the things of the flesh; but they that are after the Spirit the things of the Spirit . . . . Because the carnal mind is enmity against God: for it is not subject to the law of God, neither indeed can be" (Rom. 8: 5, 7).

Before the Spirit of God can work creatively in our hearts He must condemn and slay the "flesh" within us; that is, He must have our full consent to displace our natural self with the Person of Christ. This displacement is carefully explained in Romans 6, 7,and 8. When the seeking Christian has gone through the crucifying experience described in chapters 6 and 7 he enters into the broad, free regions of chapter 8. There self is dethroned and Christ is enthroned forever.

In the light of this it is not hard to see why the Christian's attitude toward self is such an excellent test of the validity of his religious experiences. Most of the great masters of the deeper life, such as Fenelon. Molinos, John of the Cross, Madame Guyon and a host, of others, have warned against pseudoreligious experiences that provide much carnal enjoyment but feel the flesh and puff up the heart with self-love.

A good rule is this: If this experience has served to humble me and make me little and vile in my own eyes it is of God; but if it has given me a feeling of self-satisfaction it is false and should be dismissed as emanating from self or the devil. Nothing that comes from God will minister to my pride or self-congratulation. If I am tempted to be complacent and to feel superior because I have had a remarkable vision or an advanced spiritual experience, I should go at once to my knees and repent of the whole thing. I have fallen a victim to the enemy.

5. Our relation to and our attitude toward our fellow Christians is another accurate test of religious experience.

Sometimes an earnest Christian will, after some remarkable spiritual encounter, withdraw himself from his fellow believers and develop a spirit of faultfinding. He may be honestly convinced that his experience is superior, that he is now in an advanced state of grace, and that the hoi polloi in the church where he attends are but a mixed multitude and he alone a true son of Israel. He may struggle to be patient with these religious worldlings, but his soft language and condescending smile reveal his true opinion of them-and of himself. This is a dangerous state of mind, and the more dangerous because it can justify itself by the facts. The brother has had a remarkable experience; he has received some wonderful light on the Scriptures; he has entered into a joyous land unknown to him before. And it may easily be true that the professed Christians with whom he is acquainted are worldly and dull and without spiritual enthusiasm. It is not that he is mistaken in his facts that proves him to be in error, but that his reaction to the facts is of the flesh. His new spirituality has made him less charitable.

The Lady Julian tells us in her quaint English how true Christian grace affects our attitude toward others: "For of all things the beholding and loving of the Maker maketh the soul to seem less in his own sight, and most filleth him with reverent dread and true meekness; with plenty of charity to his fellow Christians." Any religious experience that fails to deepen our love for our fellow Christians may safely be written off as spurious.

The Apostle John makes love for our fellow Christians to be a test of true faith. "My little children, let us not love in word, neither in tongue; but in deed and in truth. And hereby we know that we are of the truth, and shall assure our hearts before him" (I John 3:18, 19). Again he says, "Beloved, let us love one another: for love is of God; and every one that loveth is born of God, and knoweth God. He that loveth not knoweth not God; for God is love" (I John 4:7, 8).

As we grow in grace we grow in love toward all God's people. "Every one that loveth him that begot loveth him also that is begotten of him" (I John 5:1) . This means simply that if we love God we will love His children. All true Christian experience will deepen our love for other Christians.

Therefore we conclude that whatever tends to separate us in person or in heart from our fellow Christians is not of God, but is of the flesh or of the devil. And conversely, whatever causes us to love the children of God is likely to be of God. "By this shall all men know that ye are my disciples, if ye have love one to another" (John 13:35).

6. Another certain test of the source of religious experience is this: Note how it affects our relation to and our attitude toward the world.

By "the world" I do not mean, of course, the beautiful order of nature which God has created for the enjoyment of mankind. Neither do I mean the world of lost men in the sense used by our Lord when He said, "God so loved the world, that he gave his only begotten Son, that whosoever believeth in him should not perish, but have everlasting life. For God sent not his Son into the world to condemn the world; but that the world through him might be saved" (John 3:16, 17). Certainly any true touch of God in the soul will deepen our appreciation of the beauties of nature and intensify our love for the lost. I refer here to something else altogether.

Let an apostle say it for us: "All that is in the world, the lust of the flesh, and the lust of the eyes, and the pride of life, is not of the Father, but is of the world. And the world passeth away, and the lust thereof: but he that doeth the will of God abideth for ever" (I John 2:16, 17) .

This is the world by which we may test the spirits. It is the world of carnal enjoyments, of godless pleasures, of the pursuit of earthly riches and reputation and sinful happiness. It carries on without Christ, following the counsel of the ungodly and being animated by the prince of the power of the air, the spirit that works in the children of disobedience (Eph. 2: 2) . Its religion is a form of godliness, without power, which has a name to live but is dead. It is, in short, unregenerate human society romping on its way to hell, the exact opposite of the true Church of God, which is a society of regenerate souls going soberly but joyfully on their way to heaven.

Any real work of God in our heart will tend to unfit us for the world's fellowship. "Love not the world, neither the things that are in the world. If any man love the world, the love of the Father is not in him" (I John 2:15). "Be ye not unequally yoked together with unbelievers: for what fellowship hath righteousness with unrighteousness? and what communion hath light with darkness?" (II Cor. 6:140. It may be stated unequivocally that any spirit that permits compromise with the world is a false spirit. Any religious movement that imitates the world in any of its manifestations is false to the cross of Christ and on the side of the devil and this regardless of how much purring its leaders may do about "accepting Christ" or "letting God run your business."

7. The last test of the genuineness of Christian experience is what it does to our attitude toward sin.

The operations of grace within the heart of a believing man will turn that heart away from sin and toward holiness. "For the grace of God that bringeth salvation hath appeared to all men, teaching us that, denying ungodliness and worldly lusts, we should live soberly, righteously, and godly, in this present world; looking for that blessed hope, and the glorious appearing of the great God and our Saviour Jesus Christ" (Tit. 2:11-13) .

I do not see how it could be plainer. The same grace that saves teaches that saved man inwardly, and its teaching is both negative and positive. Negatively it teaches us to deny ungodliness and worldly lusts. Positively it teaches us to live soberly, righteously and godly right in this present world.

The man of honest heart will find no difficulty here. He has but to check his own bent to discover whether he is concerned about sin in his life more or less since the supposed work of grace was done. Anything that weakens his hatred of sin may be identified immediately as false to the Scriptures, to the Saviour and to his own soul. Whatever makes holiness more attractive and sin more intolerable may be accepted as genuine. "For thou art not a God that hath pleasure in wickedness: neither shall evil dwell with thee. The foolish shall not stand in thy sight: thou hatest all workers of iniquity" (Psa. 5: 4, 5).

Jesus warned, "There shall arise false Christs, and false prophets, and shall shew great signs and wonders; insomuch that, if it were possible, they should deceive the very elect." These words describe our day too well to be coincidental. In the hope that the "elect" may profit by them I have set forth these tests. The result is in the hand of God.

30
RELIGIOUS BOREDOM

That there is something gravely wrong with evangelical Christianity today is not likely to be denied by any serious minded person acquainted with the facts. Just what is wrong is not so easy to determine.

In examining the situation myself I find nature and reason in conflict within me, for I tend by temperament to want to settle everything with a sweep of the pen. But reason advises caution; nothing is that simple, and we must be careful to distinguish cause from effect. As every doctor knows there is a wide difference between the disease and the symptoms; and every Christian knows that there is a big difference between cause and effect in the sphere of religion.

At the root of our spiritual trouble lie a number of causes and these causes have effects, but which is cause and which effect is not always known. I suspect that many things currently under attack by our evangelists and pastors (and editors, for that matter) are not the causes of our troubles but the effects of causes that lie deeper. We treat the symptoms and wonder why the patient does not get well. Or, to change the figure, we lay down a heavy fire against nothing more substantial than the cloud of dust raised by marching enemy troops long gone by.

One mark of the low state of affairs among us is religious boredom. Whether this is a thing in itself or merely a symptom of the thing, I do not know for sure, though I suspect that it is the latter. And that it is found to some degree almost everywhere among Christians is too evident to be denied.

Boredom is, of course, a state of mind resulting from trying to maintain an interest in something that holds no trace of interest for us (the boss's jokes, say, or that lecture on the care and nurture of dahlias to which we went because we could not resist the enthusiastic urging of a friend). No one is bored by what he can in good conscience walk away from. Boredom comes when a man must try to hear with relish what for want of relish he hardly hears at all.

By this definition there is certainly much boredom in religion these days. The businessman on a Sunday morning whose mind is on golf can scarcely disguise his lack of interest in the sermon he is compelled to hear. The housewife who is unacquainted with the learned theological or philosophical jargon of the speaker; the young couple who feel a tingle of love for each other but who neither love nor know the One about whom the choir is singing-these cannot escape the low-grade mental pain we call boredom while they struggle to keep their attention focused upon the service. All these are too courteous to admit to others that they are bored and possibly too timid to admit it even to themselves, but I believe that a bit of candid confession would do us all good.

When Moses tarried in the mount, Israel became bored with the faith that sees the invisible and clamored for a god they could see and touch. And they displayed a great deal more enthusiasm for the golden calf than they did over the Lord God of Abraham. Later they tired of manna and complained against the monotony of their diet. On their petulant insistence they finally got flesh to eat, and that to their own undoing.

Those Christians who belong to the evangelical wing of the church (which I firmly believe is the only one that even approximates New Testament Christianity) have over the last half-century shown an increasing impatience with things invisible and eternal and have demanded and got a host of things visible and temporal to satisfy their fleshly appetites. Without Biblical authority, or any other right under the sun, carnal religious leaders have introduced a host of attractions that serve no purpose except to provide entertainment for the retarded saints.

It is now common practice in most evangelical churches to offer the people, especially the young people, a maximum of entertainment and a minimum of serious instruction. It is scarcely possible in most places to get anyone to attend a meeting where the only attraction is God. One can only conclude that God's professed children are bored with Him, for they must be wooed to meeting with a stick of striped candy in the form of religious movies, games and refreshments.

This has influenced the whole pattern of church life, and even brought into being a new type of church architecture, designed to house the golden calf.

So we have the strange anomaly of orthodoxy in creed and heterodoxy in practice. The striped-candy technique has been so fully integrated into our present religious thinking that it is simply taken for granted. Its victims never dream that it is not a part of the teachings of Christ and His apostles.

Any objection to the carryings on of our present golden-calf Christianity is met with the triumphant reply, "But we are winning them!" And winning them to what? To true discipleship? To cross-carrying? To self-denial? To separation from the world? To crucifixion of the flesh? To holy living? To nobility of character? To a despising of the world's treasures? To hard self-discipline? To love for God? To total committal to Christ? Of course the answer to all these questions is no.

We are paying a frightful price for our religious boredom. And that at the moment of the world's mortal peril.

31
THE CHURCH CANNOT DIE

There is a notion abroad that Christianity is on its last legs, or possibly already dead and just too weak to lie down.

This is confidently believed in Communist countries, and while spokesmen for the West are too polite to say so, one can hardly escape the feeling that they too believe the demise of the church to be a certain if embarrassing fact, the chief proof of her death being her failure to provide leadership for the world just when it needs it most.

Let me employ a pair of mixed and battered but still useful clichés and say that those who have come to bury the faith of our fathers have reckoned without the host. Just as Jesus Christ was once buried away with the full expectation that He had been gotten rid of, so His church has been laid to rest times without number; and as He disconcerted His enemies by rising from the dead so the church has confounded hers by springing again to vigorous life after all the obsequies had been performed over her coffin and the crocodile tears had been shed at her grave.

The language of devotion has helped to create the impression that the church is supposed to be a band of warriors driving the enemy before them in plain sight and with plenty of color and drama to give a pleasing flourish to the whole thing. In our hymns and pulpit oratory we have commonly pictured the church as marching along to the sound of martial music and the plaudits of the multitude.

Of course this is but a poetic figure. The individual Christian may be likened to a soldier, but the picture of the church on earth as a conquering army is not realistic. Her true situation is more accurately portrayed as a flock of sheep in the midst of wolves, or as a company of despised pilgrims plodding toward home, or as a peculiar nation protected by the Passover blood waiting for the sound of the trumpet, or as a bride looking for the coming of her bridegroom.

The world is constantly lashing the church because she has no solution for the problems of society, and the religious leaders who do not know the score wince under the lash. Every once in a while some churchman in an acute attack of conscience does penance in public for Christianity's failure to furnish bold leadership for the world in this time of crisis. "We have sinned," cries the frustrated prophet. "The world looked to us for help and we have failed it."

Well, I am all for repentance if it is genuine, and I think the church has failed, not by neglecting to provide leadership but by living too much like the world. That, however, is not what the muddled churchman means when he bares his soul in public. Rather, he erroneously assumes that the church of God has been left on earth to minister good hope and cheer to the world in such quantities that it can ignore God, reject Christ, glorify fallen human flesh and pursue its selfish ends in peace. The world wants the church to add a dainty spiritual touch to its carnal schemes, and to be there to help it to its feet and put it to bed when it comes home drunk with fleshly pleasures.

In the first place the church has received no such commission from her Lord, and in the second place the world has never shown much disposition to listen to the church when she speaks in her true prophetic voice. The attitude of the world toward the true child of God is precisely the same as that of the citizens of Vanity Fair toward Christian and his companion. "Therefore they took them and beat them, and besmeared them with dirt, and put them into the cage, that they might be made a spectacle to all men." Christian's duty was not to "provide leadership" for Vanity Fair but to keep clean from its pollution and get out of it as fast as possible. He that hath ears to hear, let him hear.

Christianity is going the way her Founder and His apostles said it would go. Its development and direction were predicted almost two thousand years ago, and this itself is a miracle. Had Christ been less than God and His apostles less than inspired they could not have foretold with such precision the state of the church so far removed from them in time and circumstance. No mortal man could have foreseen the coming of the great religiopolitical system that is Rome, or the Dark Ages, or the discovery of the New World, or the Industrial Revolution and the rise of higher criticism, or the nuclear age, and man's adventure into space. All these would have upset any human effort to foretell the religious situation these latter days; but present conditions were in fact depicted in great fullness of detail nearly two thousand years ago. Nothing unexpected has happened or is happening.

We are in real need of a reformation that will lead to revival among the churches, but the church is not dead, neither is it dying. The church cannot die.

A local church can die. This happens when all the old saints in a given place fall asleep and no young saints arise to take their place. Sometimes under these circumstances the congregation ceases to be a church, or there is no congregation left and the doors of the chapel are nailed shut. But such a condition, however deplorable, should not discourage us. The true church is the repository of the life of God among men, and if in one place the frail vessels fail, that life will break out somewhere else. Of this we may be sure.

32
THE LORDSHIP OF THE MAN
JESUS IS BASIC

We are under constant temptation these days to substitute another Christ for the Christ of the New Testament. The whole drift of modern religion is toward such a substitution.

To avoid this we must hold steadfastly to the concept of Christ as set forth so clearly and plainly in the Scriptures of truth. Though an angel from heaven should preach anything less than the Christ of the apostles let him be forthrightly and fearlessly rejected.

The mighty, revolutionary message of the Early Church was that a man named Jesus who had been crucified was now raised from the dead and exalted to the right hand of God. "Therefore let all the house of Israel know assuredly, that God hath made that same Jesus, whom ye have crucified, both Lord and Christ."

Less than three hundred years after Pentecost the hard-pressed defenders of the faith drew up a manifesto condensing those teachings of the New Testament having to do with the nature of Christ. This manifesto declares that Christ is "God of the substance of His Father, begotten before all ages: Man of the substance of His mother, born in the world: perfect God and perfect Man, of a reasonable soul and human flesh subsisting: Equal to His Father, as touching His Godhead: less than the Father, as touching His manhood. Who, although He be God and man, yet He is not two, but one Christ. One, not by conversion of the Godhead into flesh, but by the taking of the manhood into God. One altogether, not by the confusion of substance, but by the unity of Person. For as the reasonable soul and flesh is one man, so God and man is one Christ."

Even among those who acknowledge the deity of Christ there is often a failure to recognize His manhood. We are quick to assert that when He walked the earth He was God with men, but we overlook a truth equally as important, that where He sits now on His mediatorial throne He is Man with God.

The teaching of the New Testament is that now, at this very moment, there is a man in heaven appearing in the presence of God for us. He is as certainly a man as was Adam or Moses or Paul. He is a man glorified, but His glorification did not dehumanize Him. Today He is a real man, of the race of mankind, bearing our lineaments and dimensions, a visible and audible man whom any other man would recognize instantly as one of us.

But more than this, He is heir of all things, Lord of all worlds, head of the church and the first-born of the new creation. He is the way to God, the life of the believer, the hope of Israel and the high priest of every true worshiper. He holds the keys of death and hell and stands as advocate and surety for everyone who believes on Him in truth.

This is not all that can be said about Him, for were all said that might be said I suppose the world itself could not contain the books that should be written. But this in brief is the Christ we preach to sinners as their only escape from the wrath to come. With Him rest the noblest hopes and dreams of men. All the longings for immortality that rise and swell in the human breast will be fulfilled in Him or they will never know fulfillment. There is no other way (John 14:6).

Salvation comes not by "accepting the finished work" or "deciding for Christ." It comes by believing on the Lord Jesus Christ, the whole, living, victorious Lord who, as God and man, fought our fight and won it, accepted our debt as His own and paid it, took our sins and died under them and rose again to set us free. This is the true Christ, and nothing less will do.

But something less is among us, nevertheless, and we do well to identify it so that we may repudiate it. That something is a poetic fiction, a product of the romantic imagination and maudlin religious fancy. It is a Jesus, gentle, dreamy, shy, sweet, almost effeminate, and marvelously adaptable to whatever society He may find Himself in. He is cooed over by women disappointed in love, patronized by pro tem celebrities and recommended by psychiatrists as a model of a well-integrated personality. He is used as a means to almost any carnal end, but He is never acknowledged as Lord. These quasi Christians follow a quasi Christ.

They want His help but not His interference. They will flatter Him but never obey Him.

The argument of the apostles is that the Man Jesus has been made higher than angels, higher than Moses and Aaron, higher than any creature in earth or heaven. And this exalted position He attained as a man. As God He already stood infinitely above all other beings. No argument was needed to prove the transcendence of the Godhead. The apostles were not declaring the preeminence of God, which would have been superfluous, but of a man, which was necessary.

Those first Christians believed that Jesus of Nazareth, a man they knew, had been raised to a position of Lordship over the universe. He was still their friend, still one of them, but had left them for a while to appear in the presence of God on their behalf. And the proof of this was the presence of the Holy Spirit among them.

One cause of our moral weakness today is an inadequate Christology. We think of Christ as God but fail to conceive of Him as a man glorified. To recapture the power of the Early Church we must believe what they believed. And they believed they had a God-approved man representing them in heaven.

33
A DO-IT-YOURSELF EDUCATION
BETTER THAN NONE

This is written for those christians who may have missed a formal education. Let no one despair. A do-it-yourself education is better than none. It can be acquired by the proper use of our mental powers.

Our intellectual activities in the order of their importance may be graded this way: first, cogitation; second, observation; third, reading.

I wish I could include conversation in this short list. One would naturally suppose that verbal intercourse with congenial friends should be one of the most profitable of all mental activities; and it may have been so once but no more. It is now quite possible to talk for hours with civilized men and women and gain absolutely nothing from it. Conversation today is almost wholly sterile. Should the talk start on a fairly high level, it is sure within a few minutes to degenerate into cheap gossip, shoptalk, banter, weak humor, stale jokes, puns and secondhand quips. So we shall omit conversation from our list of useful intellectual activities, at least until there has been a radical reformation in the art of social discourse.

We shall not consider prayer here either, but for quite another and happier reason. Prayer is the loftiest activity possible to man, and it is of course partly mental, but it is nevertheless usually classified as a spiritual rather than an intellectual exercise; so it will be omitted.

I believe that pure thinking will do more to educate a man than any other activity he can engage in. To afford sympathetic entertainment to abstract ideas, to let one idea beget another, and that another, till the mind teems with them; to compare one idea with others, to weigh, to consider, evaluate, approve, reject, correct, refine; to join thought with thought like an architect till a noble edifice has been created within the mind; to travel back in imagination to the beginning of the creation and then to leap swiftly forward to the end of time; to bound upward through illimitable space and downward into the nucleus of an atom; and all this without so much as moving from our chair or opening the eyes-this is to soar above all the lower creation and to come near to the angels of God.

Of all earth's creatures only man can think in this way. And while thinking is the mightiest act a man can perform, perhaps for the very reason that it is the mightiest, it is the one act he likes the least and avoids most.

Aside from a few professionals, who cannot number more than one-tenth of one percent of the population, people simply do not think at all except in the most elementary way. Their thinking is done for them by the professionals.

After cogitation comes observation (in order of importance, not in order of time). Observation is, of course, simply a method of obtaining information. Without information the most powerful mind can produce nothing worthwhile. Philosophers have not agreed about whether the mind receives all of its ideas through the five senses or comes into the world with a few "innate ideas," i.e., ideas already present. But we need not settle this argument to conclude that information is indispensable to sound thought. Knowledge is the raw material out of which that finest of all machines, the mind, creates its amazing world.

The effort to think well with an empty head is sure to be largely wasted. There is nothing like a good hard fact to correct our carefully constructed theories. God has given us our five senses, and these are most highly sensitive instruments for the gathering of knowledge. So efficient are these instruments that it is quite impossible for a normal person to live even a brief time without learning something. For this reason a child five years old may properly be said to be educated in that he has by observation gathered a few facts and arranged them into some sort of orderly pattern within his mind. A doctor of philosophy has done nothing different; he has only gone a little further.

While it is impossible to live even a short time without learning something, unfortunately it is possible to live a long time and not learn very much. Observation is a powerful tool, but its usefulness depends upon how well we use it. One of the tragedies of life is that the powers of observation atrophy when not used. Just when this begins with the average person I have no sure way of knowing, but I would hazard a guess that it is at about the age of twenty-five. By that time most people have formed their habits, accepted the conventions, lost their sense of wonder and settled down to live by their glands and their appetites. For millions there is not much to observe after that but the weather and the baseball score.

Lastly reading. To think without a proper amount of good reading is to limit our thinking to our own tiny plot of ground. The crop cannot be large. To observe only and neglect reading is to deny ourselves the immense value of other people's observations; and since the better books are written by trained observers the loss is sure to be enormous. Extensive reading without the discipline of practical observation will lead to bookishness and artificiality. Reading and observing without a great deal of meditating will fill the mind with learned lumber that will always remain alien to us. Knowledge to be our own must be digested by thinking.

34
SOME THOUGHTS ON BOOKS
AND READING

One big problem in many parts of the world today is to learn how to read, and in others it is to find something to read after one has learned. In our favored West we are overwhelmed with printed matter, so the problem here becomes one of selection. We must decide what not to read.

Nearly a century ago Emerson pointed out that if it were possible for a man to begin to read the day he was born and to go on reading without interruption for seventy years, at the end of that time he would have read only enough books to fill a tiny niche in the British Library. Life is so short and the books available to us are so many that no man can possibly be acquainted with more than a fraction of one percent of the books published.

It hardly need be said that most of us are not selective enough in our reading. I have often wondered how many square yards of newsprint passes in front of the eyes of the average civilized man in the course of a year. Surely it must run into several acres; and I am afraid our average reader does not realize a very large crop on his acreage. The best advice I have heard on this topic was given by a Methodist minister. He said, "Always read your newspaper standing up." Henry David Thoreau also had a low view of the daily press. Just before leaving the city for his now celebrated sojourn on the banks of Walden Pond a friend asked him if he would like to have a newspaper delivered to his cottage. "No," replied Thoreau, "I have already seen a newspaper."

In our serious reading we are likely to be too greatly influenced by the notion that the chief value of a book is to inform; and if we were talking of textbooks of course that would be true, but when we speak or write of books we have not textbooks in mind.

The best book is not one that informs merely, but one that stirs the reader up to inform himself. The best writer is one that goes with us through the world of ideas like a friendly guide who walks beside us through the forest pointing out to us a hundred natural wonders we had not noticed before. So we learn from him to see for ourselves and soon we have no need for our guide. If he has done his work well we can go on alone and miss little as we go.

That writer does the most for us who brings to our attention thoughts that lay close to our minds waiting to be acknowledged as our own. Such a man acts as a midwife to assist at the birth of ideas that had been gestating long within our souls, but which without his help might not have been born at all.

There are few emotions so satisfying as the joy that comes from the act of recognition when we see and identify our own thoughts. We have all had teachers who sought to educate us by feeding alien ideas into our minds, ideas for which we felt no spiritual or intellectual kinship. These we dutifully tried to integrate into our total spiritual philosophy but always without success.

In a very real sense no man can teach another; he can only aid him to teach himself. Facts can be transferred from one mind to another as a copy is made from the master tape on a sound recorder. History, science, even theology, may be taught in this way, but it results in a highly artificial kind of learning and seldom has any good effect upon the deep life of the student. What the learner contributes to the learning process is fully as important as anything contributed by the teacher. If nothing is contributed by the learner the results are useless; at best there will be but the artificial creation of another teacher who can repeat the dreary work on someone else, ad infinitum.

Perception of ideas rather than the storing of them should be the aim of education. The mind should be an eye to see with rather than a bin to store facts in. The man who has been taught by the Holy Spirit will be a seer rather than a scholar. The difference is that the scholar sees and the seer sees through; and that is a mighty difference indeed.

The human intellect even in its fallen state is an awesome work of God, but it lies in darkness until it has been illuminated by the Holy Spirit. Our Lord has little good to say of the unilluminated mind, but He revels in the mind that has been renewed and enlightened by grace. He always makes the place of His feet glorious; there is scarcely anything on earth more beautiful than a Spirit-filled mind, certainly nothing more wonderful than an alert and eager mind made incandescent by the presence of the indwelling Christ.

Since what we read in a real sense enters the soul, it is vitally important that we read the best and nothing but the best. I cannot but feel that Christians were better off before there was so much reading matter to choose from. Today we must practice sharp discipline in our reading habits. Every Christian should master the Bible, or at least spend hours and days and years trying. And always he should read his Bible, as George Muller said, "with meditation."

After the Bible the next most valuable book for the Christian is a good hymnal. Let any young Christian spend a year prayerfully meditating on the hymns of Watts and Wesley alone and he will become a fine theologian. Then let him read a balanced diet of the Puritans and the Christian mystics. The results will be more wonderful than he could have dreamed.

35
THE DECLINE OF APOCALYPTIC EXPECTATION

A short generation ago, or about the time of the first World War, there was a feeling among gospel Christians that the end of the age was near, and many were breathless with anticipation of a new world order about to emerge.

This new order was to be preceded by a silent return of Christ to earth, not to remain, but to raise the righteous dead to immortality and to glorify the living saints in the twinkling of an eye. These He would catch away to the marriage supper of the Lamb, while the earth meanwhile plunged into its baptism of fire and blood in the Great Tribulation. This would be relatively brief, ending dramatically with the battle of Armageddon and the triumphant return of Christ with His Bride to reign a thousand years.

Thus the hopes and dreams of Christians were directed toward an event to be followed by a new order in which they would have a leading part. This expectation for many was so real that it quite literally determined their world outlook and way of life. One well-known and highly respected Christian leader, when handed a sum of money to pay off the mortgage on the church building, refused to use it for that purpose. Instead he used it to help send missionaries to the heathen to hasten the Lord's return. This is probably an extreme example, but it does reveal the acute apocalyptic expectation that prevailed among Christians around the time of World War I and immediately following.

Before we condemn this as extravagant we should back off a bit and try to see the whole thing in perspective. We may be wiser now (though that is open to serious question), but those Christians had something very wonderful which we today lack. They had a unifying hope; we have none. Their activities were concentrated; ours are scattered, overlapping and often self-defeating. They fully expected to win; we are not even sure we know what "win" means. Our Christian hope has been subjected to so much examination, analysis and revision that we are embarrassed to admit that we have such a hope at all.

And those expectant believers were not wholly wrong. They were only wrong about the time. They saw Christ's triumph as being nearer than it was, and for that reason their timing was off; but their hope itself was valid. Many of us have had the experience of misjudging the distance of a mountain toward which we were traveling. The huge bulk that loomed against the sky seemed very near, and it was hard to persuade ourselves that it was not receding as we approached. So the City of God appears so large to the minds of the world-weary pilgrim that he is sometimes the innocent victim of an optical illusion; and he may be more than a little disappointed when the glory seems to move farther away as he approaches.

But the mountain is there; the traveler need only press on to reach it. And the Christian's hope is there too; his judgment is not always too sharp, but he is not mistaken in the long view; he will see the glory in God's own time.

We evangelicals have become sophisticated, blasé. We have lost what someone called the "millennial component" from our Christian faith. To escape what we believe to be the slough of a mistaken hope we have detoured far out into the wilderness of complete hopelessness.

Christians now chatter learnedly about things simple believers have always taken for granted. They are on the defensive, trying to prove things that a previous generation never doubted. We have allowed unbelievers to get us in a corner and have given them the advantage by permitting them to choose the time and place of encounter. We smart under the attack of the quasi-Christian unbeliever, and the nervous, self-conscious defense we make is called "the religious dialogue."

Under the scornful attack of the religious critic real Christians who ought to know better are now "rethinking" their faith. Scarcely anything has escaped the analysts. With a Freudian microscope they examine everything: foreign missions, the Book of Genesis. the inspiration of the Scriptures, morals, all tried and proven methods, polygamy, liquor, sex, prayer-all have come in for inquisition by those who engage in the contemporary dialogue. Adoration has given way to celebration in the holy place, if indeed any holy place remains to this generation of confused Christians. The causes of the decline of apocalyptic expectation are many, not the least being the affluent society in which we live. If the rich man with difficulty enters the kingdom of God, then it would be logical to conclude that a society having the highest percentage of well-to-do persons in it would have the lowest percentage of Christians, all things else being equal. If the "deceitfulness of riches" chokes the Word and makes it unfruitful, then this would be the day of near-fruitless preaching, at least in the opulent West. And if surfeiting and drunkenness and worldly cares tend to unfit the Christian for the coming of Christ, then this generation of Christians should be the least prepared for that event.

On the North American continent Christianity has become the religion of the prosperous middle and upper classes almost entirely, the very rich or the very poor rarely become practicing Christians. The touching picture of the poorly dressed, hungry saint, clutching his Bible under his arm and with the light of God shining in his face hobbling painfully toward the church, is chiefly imaginary. One of the biggest problems of even the most ardent Christian these days is to find a parking place for the shiny chariot that transports him effortlessly to the house of God where he hopes to prepare his soul for the world to come.

In the United States and Canada the middle class today possesses more earthly goods and lives in greater luxury than emperors and maharajas did a short century ago. And since the bulk of Christians comes from this class it is not difficult to see why the apocalyptic hope has all but disappeared from among us. It is hard to focus attention upon a better world to come when a more comfortable one than this can hardly be imagined. The best we can do is to look for heaven after we have revelled for a lifetime in the luxuries of a fabulously generous earth. As long as science can make us so cozy in this present world it is hard to work up much pleasurable anticipation of a new world order.

But affluence is only one cause of the decline of the apocalyptic hope. There are other and more important ones.

The whole problem is a big one, a theological one, a moral one. An inadequate view of Christ may be the chief trouble. Christ has been explained, humanized, demoted. Many professed Christians no longer expect Him to usher in a new order; they are not at all sure that He is able to do so; or if He does, it will be with the help of art, education, science and technology; that is, with the help of man. This revised expectation amounts to disillusionment for many. And of course no one can become too radiantly happy over a King of kings who has been stripped of His crown or a Lord of lords who has lost His sovereignty.

Another cause of the decline of expectation is hope deferred which, according to the proverb, "maketh the heart sick." The modern civilized man is impatient; he takes the short-range view of things. He is surrounded by gadgets that get things done in a hurry. He was brought up on quick oats; he likes his instant coffee; he wears drip-dry shirts and takes one-minute Polaroid snapshots of his children. His wife shops for her spring hat before the leaves are down in the fall. His new car, if he buys it after June 1, is already an old model when he brings it home. He is almost always in a hurry and can't bear to wait for anything.

This breathless way of living naturally makes for a mentality impatient of delay, and when this man enters the kingdom of God he brings his short-range psychology with him. He finds prophecy too slow for him. His first radiant expectations soon lose their luster. He is likely to inquire, "Lord, wilt thou at this time restore again the kingdom to Israel?" and when there is no immediate response he may conclude, "My lord delayeth his coming." The faith of Christ offers no buttons to push for quick service. The new order must wait the Lord's own time, and that is too much for the man in a hurry. He just gives up and becomes interested in something else.

Another cause is eschatological confusion. The vitalizing hope of the emergence of a new world wherein dwelleth righteousness became an early casualty in the war of conflicting prophetic interpretations. Teachers of prophecy, who knew more than the prophets they claimed to teach, debated the fine points of Scripture ad infinitum while a discouraged and disillusioned Christian public shook their heads and wondered. A leader of one evangelical group told me that his denomination had recently been, in his words, "split down the middle" over a certain small point of prophetic teaching, one incidentally which had never been heard of among the children of God until about one hundred years ago.

Certain popular views of prophecy have been discredited by events within the lifetime of some of us; a new generation of Christians cannot be blamed if their Messianic expectations are somewhat confused. When the teachers are divided, what can the pupils do?

It should be noted that there is a vast difference between the doctrine of Christ's coming and the hope of His coming. The first we may hold without feeling a trace of the second. Indeed there are multitudes of Christians today who hold the doctrine of the second coming. What I have talked about here is that overwhelming sense of anticipation that lifts the life onto a new plane and fills the heart with rapturous optimism. This is what we today lack.

Frankly, I do not know whether or not it is possible to recapture the spirit of anticipation that animated the Early Church and cheered the hearts of gospel Christians only a few decades ago. Certainly scolding will not bring it back, nor arguing over prophecy, nor condemning those who do not agree with us. We may do all or any of these things without arousing the desired spirit of joyous expectation. That unifying, healing, purifying hope is for the childlike, the innocent-hearted, the unsophisticated.

Possibly nothing short of a world catastrophe that will destroy every false trust and turn our eyes once more upon the Man Christ Jesus will bring back the glorious hope to a generation that has lost it.

36
CHOICES REVEAL – AND MAKE – CHARACTER

Into nine words, having altogether but eleven syllables, Luke packs a world of universal truth: "Being let go, they went to their own company" (Acts 4:23).

Every normal man has a "company," however small, where he feels at home and to which he will return when he is tired of being alone. The important thing about a man is not where he goes when he is compelled to go, but where he goes when he is free to go where he will. The apostles went to jail, and that is not too revealing because they went there against their will; but when they got out of jail and could go where they would they immediately went to the praying company. From this we learn a great deal about them. The choices of life, not the compulsions, reveal character.

A man is absent from church Sunday morning. Where is he? If he is in a hospital having his appendix removed his absence tells us nothing about him except that he is ill; but if he is out on the golf course, that tells us a lot. To go to the hospital is compulsory; to go to the golf course, voluntary. The man is free to choose and he chooses to play instead of to pray. His choice reveals what kind of man he is. Choices always do.

The difference between a slave society and a free one lies in the number of free acts possible in each as compared with acts of compulsion. No society is wholly slave, as none is wholly free, but in a free society the voluntary choices are at a maximum and the acts of compulsion relatively few. In the slave society the proportions are exactly reversed.

The true character of a people is revealed in the uses it makes of its freedoms. The slave peoples do what they are told because they are not free to do what they will. It is the free nation that reveals its character by its voluntary choices. The man who "bowed by the weight of centuries . . . leans upon his hoe and gazes on the ground" when the long day's work is over is glad to get home to supper and to bed; he has little time for anything else. But in those fortunate lands where modern machinery and labor unions have given men many free hours out of every day and at least two free days out of every week, they have time to do almost anything they will. They are free to destroy themselves by their choices, and many of them are doing just that.

There is always danger that a free nation may imperil its freedom by a series of small choices destructive of that freedom. The liberty the fathers won in blood the sons may toss away in prodigality and debilitating pleasures. Any nation which for an extended period puts pleasure before liberty is likely to lose the liberty it misused.

In the realm of religion right choices are critically important. If we Protestant Christians would retain our freedom we dare not abuse it, and it is always to abuse freedom when we choose the easy way rather than the harder but better way. The casual indifference with which millions of Protestants view their God-blessed religious liberty is ominous. Being let go they go on weekends to the lakes and mountains and beaches to play shuffleboard, fish and sun bathe. They go where their heart is and come back to the praying company only when the bad weather drives them in. Let this continue long enough and evangelical Protestantism will be ripe for a take-over by Rome.

The Christian gospel is a message of freedom through grace and we must stand fast in the liberty wherewith Christ has made us free. But what shall we do with our freedom? The Apostle Paul grieved that some of the believers of his day took advantage of their freedom and indulged the flesh in the name of Christian liberty. They threw off discipline, scorned obedience and made gods of their own bellies. It is not difficult to decide which company such as these belonged to. They revealed it by the company they kept.

Our choices reveal what kind of persons we are, but there is another side to the coin. We may by our choices also determine what kind of persons we will become. We humans are not only in a state of being, we are in a state of becoming; we are on a slow spiral moving gradually up or down. Here we move not singly but in companies, and we are drawn to these companies by the attraction of similarity.

I think it might be well for us to check our spiritual condition occasionally by the simple test of compatibility. When we are free to go, where do we go? In what company do we feel most at home? Where do our thoughts turn when they are free to turn where they will? When the pressure of work or business or school has temporarily lifted and we are able to think of what we will instead of what we must, what do we think of then?

The answer to these questions may tell us more about ourselves than we can comfortably accept. But we had better face up to things. We haven't too much time at the most.

37
THE IMPORTANCE OF SOUND DOCTRINE

It would be impossible to overemphasize the importance of sound doctrine in the life of a Christian. Right thinking about all spiritual matters is imperative if we would have right living. As men do not gather grapes of thorns nor figs of thistles, sound character does not grow out of unsound teaching.

The word doctrine means simply religious beliefs held and taught. It is the sacred task of all Christians, first as believers and then as teachers of religious beliefs, to be certain that these beliefs correspond exactly to truth. A precise agreement between belief and fact constitutes soundness in doctrine. We cannot afford to have less.

The apostles not only taught truth but contended for its purity against any who would corrupt it. The Pauline epistles resist every effort of false teachers to introduce doctrinal vagaries. John's epistles are sharp with condemnation of those teachers who harassed the young church by denying the incarnation and throwing doubts upon the doctrine of the Trinity; and Jude in his brief but powerful epistle rises to heights of burning eloquence as he pours scorn upon evil teachers who would mislead the saints.

Each generation of Christians must look to its beliefs. While truth itself is unchanging, the minds of men are porous vessels out of which truth can leak and into which error may seep to dilute the truth they contain. The human heart is heretical by nature and runs to error as naturally as a garden to weeds. All a man, a church or a denomination needs to guarantee deterioration of doctrine is to take everything for granted and do nothing. The unattended garden will soon be overrun with weeds;

the heart that fails to cultivate truth and root out error will shortly be a theological wilderness; the church or denomination that grows careless on the highway of truth will before long find itself astray, bogged down in some mud flat from which there is no escape.

In every field of human thought and activity accuracy is considered a virtue. To err ever so slightly is to invite serious loss, if not death itself. Only in religious thought is faithfulness to truth looked upon as a fault. When men deal with things earthly and temporal they demand truth; when they come to the consideration of things heavenly and eternal they hedge and hesitate as if truth either could not be discovered or didn't matter anyway.

Montaigne said that a liar is one who is brave toward God and a coward toward men; for a liar faces God and shrinks from men. Is this not simply a proof of unbelief? Is it not to say that the liar believes in men but is not convinced of the existence of God, and is willing to risk the displeasure of a God who may not exist rather than that of man who obviously does?

I think also that deep, basic unbelief is back of human carelessness in religion. The scientist, the physician, the navigator deals with matters he knows are real; and because these things are real the world demands that both teacher and practitioner be skilled in the knowledge of them. The teacher of spiritual things only is required to be unsure in his beliefs, ambiguous in his remarks and tolerant of every religious opinion expressed by anyone, even by the man least qualified to hold an opinion.

Haziness of doctrine has always been the mark of the liberal. When the Holy Scriptures are rejected as the final authority on religious belief something must be found to take their place. Historically that something has been either reason or sentiment: if sentiment, it has been humanism. Sometimes there has been an admixture of the two, as may be seen in liberal churches today. These will not quite give up the Bible, neither will they quite believe it; the result is an unclear body of beliefs more like a fog than a mountain, where anything may be true but nothing may be trusted as being certainly true.

We have gotten accustomed to the blurred puffs of gray fog that pass for doctrine in modernistic churches and expect nothing better, but it is a cause for real alarm that the fog has begun of late to creep into many evangelical churches. From some previously unimpeachable sources are now coming vague statements consisting of a milky admixture of

Scripture, science and human sentiment that is true to none of its ingredients because each one works to cancel the others out.

Certain of our evangelical brethren appear to be laboring under the impression that they are advanced thinkers because they are rethinking evolution and reevaluating various Bible doctrines or even divine inspiration itself; but so far are they from being advanced thinkers that they are merely timid followers of modernism-fifty years behind the parade.

Little by little evangelical Christians these days are being brainwashed. One evidence is that increasing numbers of them are becoming ashamed to be found unequivocally on the side of truth. They say they believe but their beliefs have been so diluted as to be impossible of clear definition.

Moral power has always accompanied definitive beliefs. Great saints have always been dogmatic. We need right now a return to a gentle dogmatism that smiles while it stands stubborn and firm on the Word of God that liveth and abideth forever.

38
SOME THINGS ARE NOT NEGOTIABLE

W ill Rogers once opined that a sure way to prevent war would be to abolish peace conferences.

Of course Will, as usual, had his tongue in his cheek; he meant only to poke fun at the weak habit of substituting talk for action. Still there is more than a little uncomfortable truth in his remark.

This above all others is the age of much talk. Hardly a day passes that the newspapers do not carry one or another of the headlines "Talks to Begin" or "Talks to Continue" or "Talks to Resume." The notion back of this endless official chatter is that all differences between men result from their failure to understand each other; if each can discover exactly what the other thinks they will find to their delight that they are really in full agreement after all. Then they have only to smile, shake hands, go home and live happily ever after.

At the bottom of all this is the glutenous, one-world, all-men-are-brothers philosophy that has taken such hold on the minds of many of our educators and politicians. (The hardheaded realists of the Communist camp know better; maybe that is why they are makingsuch alarming advances throughout the world while the all-men-are-brothers devotees are running around in confusion, trying to keep smiling if it kills them.)

Tolerance, charity, understanding, good will, patience and other such words and ideas are lifted from the Bible, misunderstood and applied indiscriminately to every situation. The kidnaper will not steal your baby if you only try to understand him; the burglar caught sneaking into your house with a gun is not really bad; he is just hungry for fellowship and togetherness; the gang killer taking his victim for a oneway ride can be dissuaded from committing murder if someone will only have faith in his basic goodness and have a talk with him. And this is supposed to be the teaching of Jesus, which it most certainly is not.

The big thing now is to "keep in touch." Never let the dialogue die and never accept any decision as final; everything can be negotiated. Where there is life there is talk and where there is talk there is hope. "As long as they are talking they are not shooting at each other," say the advocates of the long palaver, and in so saying they forget Pearl Harbor.

This yen to confer has hit the church also, which is not strange since almost everything the church is doing these days has been suggested to her by the world. I observe with pained amusement how many water boys of the pulpit in their effort to be prophets are standing up straight and tall and speaking out boldly in favor of ideas that have been previously fed into their minds by the psychiatrists, the sociologists, the novelists, the scientists and the secular educators. The ability to appraise correctly the direction public opinion is moving is a gift not to be despised; by means of it we preachers can talk loudly and still stay out of trouble.

A new Decalogue has been adopted by the neo-Christians of our day, the first word of which reads "Thou shalt not disagree"; and a new set of Beatitudes too, which begins "Blessed are they that tolerate everything, for they shall not be made accountable for anything." It is now the accepted thing to talk over religious differences in public with the understanding that no one will try to convert another or point out errors in his belief. The purpose of these talks is not to confront truth, but to discover how the followers of other religions think and thus benefit from their views as we hope they will from ours.

It is a truism that people agree to disagree only about matters they consider unimportant. No man is tolerant when it concerns his life or the life of his child, and no one will agree to negotiate over any religious matter he considers vital to his eternal welfare. Imagine Moses agreeing to take part in a panel discussion with Israel over the golden calf; or Elijah engaging in a gentlemanly dialogue with the prophets of Baal. Or try to picture our Lord Jesus Christ seeking a meeting of minds with the Pharisees to iron out differences; or Athanasius trying to rise above his differences with Arius in order to achieve union on a higher level; or Luther crawling into the presence of the pope in the name of a broader Christian fellowship.

The desire to be liked even if not respected is a great weakness in any man's character, and in that of a minister of Jesus Christ it is a weakness wholly inexcusable. The popular image of the man of God as a smiling, congenial, asexual religious mascot whose handshake is always soft and whose head is always bobbing in the perpetual Yes of universal acquiescence is not the image found in the Scriptures of truth.

The blessing of God is promised to the peacemaker, but the religious negotiator had better watch his step. The ability to settle quarrels between members of God's household is a heavenly gift and one that should be assiduously cultivated. The discerning soul who can reconcile separated friends by prayer and appeal to the Scriptures is worth his weight in diamonds.

That is one thing, but the effort to achieve unity at the expense of truth and righteousness is another. To seek to be friends with those who will not be the friends of Christ is to be a traitor to our Lord. Darkness and light can never be brought together by talk. Some things are not negotiable.

39
THE SAINT MUST WALK ALONE

Most of the world's great souls have been lonely. Loneliness seems to be one price the saint must pay for his saintliness.

In the morning of the world (or should we say, in that strange darkness that came soon after the dawn of man's creation) that pious soul, Enoch, walked with God and was not, for God took him; and while it is not stated in so many words, a fair inference is that Enoch walked a path quite apart from his contemporaries.

Another lonely man was Noah who, of all the antediluvians, found grace in the sight of God; and every shred of evidence points to the aloneness of his life even while surrounded by his people.

Again, Abraham had Sarah and Lot, as well as many servants and herdmen, but who can read his story and the apostolic comment upon it without sensing instantly that he was a man "whose soul was alike a star and dwelt apart"? As far as we know not one word did God ever speak to him in the company of men. Face down he communed with his God, and the innate dignity of the man forbade that he assume this posture in the presence of others. How sweet and solemn was the scene that night of the sacrifice when he saw the lamps of fire moving between the pieces of offering. There alone with a horror of great darkness upon him he heard the voice of God and knew that he was a man marked for divine favor.

Moses also was a man apart. While yet attached to the court of Pharaoh he took long walks alone, and during one of these walks while far removed from the crowds he saw an Egyptian and a Hebrew fighting and came to the rescue of his countryman. After the resultant break with Egypt he dwelt in almost complete seclusion in the desert. There while he watched his sheep alone the wonder of the burning bush appeared to him, and later on the peak of Sinai he crouched alone to gaze in fascinated awe at the Presence, partly hidden, partly disclosed, within the cloud and fire.

The prophets of pre-Christian times differed widely from each other, but one mark they bore in common was their enforced loneliness. They loved their people and gloried in the religion of the fathers, but their loyalty to the God of Abraham, Isaac and Jacob, and their zeal for the welfare of the nation of Israel drove them away from the crowd and into long periods of heaviness. "I am become a stranger unto my brethren, and an alien unto my mother's children," cried one and unwittingly spoke for all the rest.

Most revealing of all is the sight of that One of whom Moses and all the prophets did write treading His lonely way to the cross, His deep loneliness unrelieved by the presence of the multitudes.

> 'Tis midnight, and on Olive's brow
> The star is dimmed that lately shone;
> 'Tis midnight; in the garden now,
> The suffering Saviour prays alone.
> 'Tis midnight, and from all removed
> The Saviour wrestles lone with fears,
> E'en the disciple whom He loved
> Heeds not his Master's grief and tears.
> —William B. Tappan

He died alone in the darkness hidden from the sight of mortal man and no one saw Him when He arose triumphant and walked out of the tomb, though many saw Him afterward and bore witness to what they saw.

There are some things too sacred for any eye but God's to look upon. The curiosity, the clamor, the well-meant but blundering effort to help can only hinder the waiting soul and make unlikely if not impossible the communication of the secret message of God to the worshiping heart.

Sometimes we react by a kind of religious reflex and repeat dutifully the proper words and phrases even though they fail to express our real feelings and lack the authenticity of personal experience. Right now is such a time. A certain conventional loyalty may lead some who hear this unfamiliar truth expressed for the first time to say brightly, "Oh, I am never lonely. Christ said, `I will never leave you nor forsake you,' and, `Lo, I am with you alway.' How can I be lonely when Jesus is with me?"

Now I do not want to reflect on the sincerity of any Christian soul, but this stock testimony is too neat to be real. It is obviously what the speaker thinks should be true rather than what he has proved to be true by the test of experience. This cheerful denial of loneliness proves only that the speaker has never walked with God without the support and encouragement afforded him by society. The sense of companionship which he mistakenly attributes to the presence of Christ may and probably does arise from the presence of friendly people. Always remember: you cannot carry a cross in company. Though a man were surrounded by a vast crowd, his cross is his alone and his carrying of it marks him as a man apart. Society has turned against him; otherwise he would have no cross. No one is a friend to the man with a cross. "They all forsook him, and fled."

The pain of loneliness arises from the constitution of our nature. God made us for each other. The desire for human companionship is completely natural and right. The loneliness of the Christian results from his walk with God in an ungodly world, a walk that must often take him away from the fellowship of good Christians as well as from that of the unregenerate world. His Godgiven instincts cry out for companionship with others of his kind, others who can understand his longings, his aspirations, his absorption in the love of Christ; and because within his circle of friends there are so few who share his inner experiences he is forced to walk alone. The unsatisfied longings of the prophets for human understanding caused them to cry out in their complaint, and even our Lord Himself suffered in the same way.

The man who has passed on into the divine Presence in actual inner experience will not find many who understand him. A certain amount of social fellowship will of course be his as he mingles with religious persons in the regular activities of the church, but true spiritual fellowship will be hard to find. But he should not expect things to be otherwise. After all, he is a stranger and a pilgrim, and the journey he takes is not on his feet but in his heart. He walks with God in the garden of his own souland who but God can walk there with him? He is of another spirit from the multitudes that tread the courts of the Lord's house. He has seen that of which they have only heard, and he walks among them somewhat as Zacharias walked after his return from the altar when the people whispered, "He has seen a vision."

The truly spiritual man is indeed something of an oddity. He lives not for himself but to promote the interests of Another. He seeks to persuade people to give all to his Lord and asks no portion or share for himself. He delights not to be honored but to see his Saviour glorified in the eyes of men. His joy is to see his Lord promoted and himself neglected. He finds few who care to talk about that which is the supreme object of his interest, so he is often silent and preoccupied in the midst of noisy religious shoptalk. For this he earns the reputation of being dull and overserious, so he is avoided and the gulf between him and society widens. He searches for friends upon whose garments he can detect the smell of myrrh and aloes and cassia out of the ivory palaces, and finding few or none he, like Mary of old, keeps these things in his heart.

It is this very loneliness that throws him back upon God. "When my father and my mother forsake me, then the Lord will take me up." His inability to find human companionship drives him to seek in God what he can find nowhere else. He learns in inner solitude what he could not have learned in the crowd that Christ is All in All, that He is made unto us wisdom, righteousness, sanctification and redemption, that in Him we have and possess life's *summum bonum*.

Two things remain to be said. One, that the lonely man of whom we speak is not a haughty man, nor is he the holier-than-thou, austere saint so bitterly satirized in popular literature. He is likely to feel that he is the least of all men and is sure to blame himself for his very loneliness. He wants to share his feelings with others and to open his heart to some like-minded soul who will understand him, but the spiritual climate around him does not encourage it, so he remains silent and tells his griefs to God alone.

The second thing is that the lonely saint is not the withdrawn man who hardens himself against human suffering and spends his days contemplating the heavens. Just the opposite is true. His loneliness makes him sympathetic to the approach of the broken-hearted and the fallen and the sin-bruised. Because he is detached from the world he is all the more able to help it. Meister Eckhart taught his followers that if they should find themselves in prayer as it were caught up to the third heavens and happen to remember that a poor widow needed food, they should break off the prayer instantly and go care for the widow. "God will not suffer you to lose anything by it," he told them. "You can take up again in prayer where you left off and the Lord will make it up to you." This is typical of the great mystics and masters of the interior life from Paul to the present day.

The weakness of so many modern Christians is that they feel too much at home in the world. In their effort to achieve restful "adjustment" to unregenerate society they have lost their pilgrim character and become an essential part of the very moral order against which they are sent to protest. The world recognizes them and accepts them for what they are. And this is the saddest thing that can be said about them. They are not lonely, but neither are they saints.

41358973R00126

Made in the USA
Lexington, KY
10 May 2015